ONCE A PARATROOPER

The Story of a Lone Soldier in the Gaza War

IRA KOHLER

Foreword by Orna & Ronen Neutra

PARATROOPER PRESS

Published by Paratrooper Press

Produced by GMK Writing and Editing, Inc.
Managing Editor: Katie Benoit
Developmental Editor: Randy Ladenheim-Gil
Copyedited by Kelly Nutter Clody
Proofread by Elizabeth Crooks
Text composition by Libby Kingsbury
Cover and interior design by Vicky Vaughn Shea
Printed by IngramSpark

Print ISBN: 978-1-966981-28-2
Ebook EISN: 978-1-966981-29-9

Visit the author at irakohler.com

Note from Author:
The author has made every effort to ensure accuracy. Any errors or omissions are purely accidental and inadvertent. The descriptions and accounts described herein are exclusively from his personal experiences and perspective. The author acknowledges that others may have differing memories and/or points of view.

ADVANCE PRAISE FOR ONCE A PARATROOPER

"In *Once a Paratrooper*, Ira Kohler presents a gripping and inspiring account of his service as an American without family members living in Israel—a Lone Soldier—fighting in the Gaza War. For supporters of Israel and those wishing to know the truth about the Gaza War, Kohler's memoir is an essential source."

—**Michael Oren**, former Israeli Ambassador to the United States and Member of Knesset, author of *Six Days of War*

"Ira Kohler chose to leave his home in New York and come to Israel as a Lone Soldier, driven by a desire to contribute to the country and fulfill the Jewish and Zionist values he was raised on. He writes about the hardships of grueling combat service and the disconnect from family and friends back across the ocean. Despite these challenges, as described in the book, Ira successfully completed a full term of service in the Paratroopers Brigade, during which he took part in the battle of Kibbutz Be'eri and the war in the Gaza Strip."

—**Major General (Res.) Doron Almog**, Chairman of the Executive of The Jewish Agency for Israel & Chairman of ADI Negev-Nahalat Eran

"This moving, inspiring book tracks the extraordinary story of a Jewish kid from Long Island who helped save Israel, the Jewish people, and the world as an Israeli soldier on October 7th and thereafter. Ira Kohler does a magnificent job of capturing the chaos, the fear, the grit, the smell, and the casual courage he and his fellow soldiers experienced every day while facing unprecedented challenges in battle. The book is not only compelling and easy-to-read, but it's also hard to put down and even harder to forget."

—**Professor Gil Troy**, author of *The Zionist Ideas*

"Ira tells an inspiring story of a young man from Long Island, New York, serving in the IDF and fighting on the front lines on October 7th and in Gaza. This book takes the reader into the emotions and challenges of a soldier during the toughest moments and highlights the powerful connection between Ira and his friend, Omer Neutra, both constituents of mine, as he fought to bring him home from Hamas captivity."

—**Rep. Tom Suozzi**, Congressman, New York's 3rd
Congressional District

To Amir Naim, Omer Neutra, and Yair Avitan…
three friends lost in the war

Amir Naim, Omer Neutra, and Yair Avitan
Courtesy Ira Kohler

CONTENTS

OPENING REMARKS

by Major General (Res.) Doron Almog

Nearly sixty years ago, as a young man, I chose to enlist in the paratroopers. My early years in the paratroopers were years of daring operations and harsh warfare. Fighting against the Egyptian commando on the Shadwan Island, eliminating the terrorists behind the Israeli Olympians massacre in Munich during the operation in Tripoli, the Yom Kippur War—the earthquake of my generation, Operation Entebbe for the rescue of 105 hostages 4,000 kilometers away from Israel. Great pride alongside deep pain for the many of my generation who fell in battle, among them my brother, Eran, who fell defending The Golan Heights during the Yom Kippur War.

For me, the paratroopers were the melting pot of the values that shaped my life. Courage, friendship, tenacity, creativity, subterfuge, and devotion to the mission. Willingness to sacrifice for the one and only Jewish state. Developing a sense of competence: that nobody can overcome us, that we are the strongest, that we never surrender and always emerge victorious, even in the darkest of hours. And, alongside all these, continued my combat service with an oath to my brother, Eran: never leave a bleeding soldier behind. A personal oath shaped and inspired by my upbringing in the paratroopers.

In the paratroopers I learned leadership through the soles of my boots. From a squad commander to the commander of the red brigade, paratroopers officer and chief infantry officer, commander of the Gaza division, head of the IDF Southern Command.

Hundreds of battles. Trials of fire, command, and leadership.

The paratroopers is where I learned just how important comradeship is among soldiers. How vital is that unique, one-of-a-kind bond between a commander and those he commands. The paratroopers is where I also met the fear, pain, and loss, and, alongside these, the necessity of pressing forward despite the hardships and the void left in the heart by the loss of brothers-in-arms. Serving in the paratroopers shaped my character and, to great extent, remains present in my life to this day. Once a paratrooper, always a paratrooper.

Ira Kohler chose to leave his home in New York and come to Israel as a Lone Soldier, driven by a desire to contribute to the country and fulfill the Jewish and Zionist values he was raised on. He writes about the hardships of grueling combat service and the disconnect from family and friends back across the ocean. Despite these challenges, as described in the book, Ira successfully completed a full term of service in the paratroopers brigade, during which he took part in the battle of Kibbutz Be'eri and the war in the Gaza Strip.

Ira chose to dedicate this book to his brothers-in-arms who fell in the war: Captain Omer Neutra—also a Lone Soldier—who fell in battle between Nirim and Nir Oz on October 7th and whose body was kidnapped to Gaza; Major (Res.) Amir Naim, who fell on October 7th while defending his home in Kibbutz Erez; and Staff Sergeant Yair Avitan, who fell during the war in combat against terrorists in the Shejaiya neighborhood in the northern Gaza Strip. In their lives and in their deaths, Ira and his friends represent Zionism at its finest and the unique friendship forged here between those born in Israel and those born in the diaspora, city dwellers and kibbutz residents, religious and secular alike. All underwent a significant melting pot within the paratroopers. A bond of comradeship for a lifetime.

Once a Paratrooper leads the reader toward an understanding of the second part of the paratrooper's slogan, "Always a Paratrooper." Just as I did years ago, Ira and his friends today experience hardships while rising to the challenges. They are the ultimate expression of the society we all strive to live in: "A Model Society."

—Major General (Res.) Doron Almog
Chairman of the Executive of The Jewish Agency for Israel
Chairman of ADI Negev-Nahalat Eran

FOREWORD

by Orna & Ronen Neutra

Ira and Omer grew up in the same Long Island community. They shared schools, sports, camps, and the steady rhythms of Jewish communal life. From the outside, their childhoods looked very similar. Both were born and raised in New York, shaped by strong education and a deep exposure to Jewish and Zionist values. There were differences, but they were matters of background not belief. We are Israeli. Omer was born and raised in the United States, but Israel was always present in our home—through language, family, and lived connection. And while Ira's parents are not Israeli, his connection to Israel was built through education, community, and experience. Not inherited but absorbed. What mattered most is that both young men arrived at their decisions to enlist in the IDF deliberately.

Neither Ira nor Omer stumbled into service. Both understood what it meant. Their choices were extraordinary not because of a single defining moment but because of a lifelong journey—shaped by schools, youth movements, camps, friendships, travel, and a deep sense that Israel was not abstract or distant but personal and demanding of responsibility.

Ira knew he wanted to serve years before he made *aliyah*. We followed his path as he finished college and prepared himself for what he knew was coming. His parents shared his decision with us—with pride and with understandable apprehension. We recognized both emotions immediately.

When Ira moved to Israel and enlisted, we followed his journey closely. He was not our son, but he was someone we cared about deeply—someone our son cared about deeply. We hoped his service would be meaningful and that, when it ended, he would return home safely.

October 7th changed everything.

As the horror of that day unfolded, we—Omer's parents—and Ira's parents were together in New York, watching events unfold in real time. We followed the news minute by minute, translating Hebrew WhatsApp messages into English for Ira's parents as information poured in faster than it could be understood. We learned that Omer's group had been attacked. We wrote letters to the White House seeking information, made phone calls to our representatives, and tried to comprehend the scale of what had happened.

In those early days, we held two prayers at once: We prayed for Omer to be found alive. And we prayed for Ira—that he would complete his service and return home whole. Physically. Mentally. Spiritually. Day after day we waited for news. For clarity. For the war to end.

This book is Ira's firsthand account of what it means to take part in war—not as a symbol, not as an idea, but as a human being in his early twenties. He writes about the dilemmas, the encounters, the fear, the exhaustion, and about the moments of gratitude—gratitude for surviving and for saving lives. He does not write as an observer. He writes as someone who was there.

Ira shows what IDF soldiers actually are: young people carrying responsibility far heavier than their years. They are not monsters. They are not abstractions. They are individuals making impossible decisions under fire, guided by a clear sense of responsibility to protect their people.

Ira also shows, clearly and without exaggeration, what this war was. He saw firsthand how terrorists struck peace-seeking communities. He describes a reality in which terrorists used civilians as human shields, held hostages—innocent civilians made up of women and children and the elderly—and used our loved ones as bargaining chips.

This is the war that ended Omer's life.

That truth matters.

Omer appears in this book not as a headline or a cause but as a person Ira knew well—a childhood friend, a peer, someone whose absence was felt every day.

Reading this manuscript was painful for us. It brought us back to moments that remain very raw. But it also reinforced the importance of telling these stories honestly. Not to provoke, not to persuade, but to bear witness.

We are deeply grateful to Ira for carrying Omer's story forward and for sharing it with those he has met since completing his service. By doing so, Ira has ensured that Omer is remembered not only for how he died but for who he was and for the world that shaped him.

This book does not offer closure. What it offers instead is truth—told carefully, responsibly, and humanly.

We are grateful to Ira for telling it. And for carrying Omer with him—not as a symbol but as a friend.

—Orna and Ronen Neutra

PROLOGUE

To my left sat a friend, and to my right, my commander. We sat shoulder to shoulder on the benches of a helicopter. Between them, I held my 7.6-kilogram Negev machine gun, snug between my legs, the only thing keeping my knees apart. On the ground lay my war bag—the same one I had packed a week earlier preparing for a war exercise. Now, it was prepared for real war. Inside were hundreds of bullets, six liters of water, a change of clothes, a small amount of food, my *naknash* gear for cleaning my gun, and other essentials. With my helmet buckled under my chin, protective glasses on my eyes, and kneepads strapped tight, I was fully geared for battle.

The helicopter's benches ran along both sides, leaving an open alleyway in the middle. I sat crammed between soldiers, with more seated across from me, and more piled on top of each other in the alleyway, pressing against those of us on the benches. My legs were pinned, and a cramp started to form—a minor discomfort in the gravity of the moment.

The wait to depart was excruciating. Finally, the back door closed, the propellers roared, and the helicopter lifted off. Windows lined the chopper with stunning views below, and I extended my neck for glimpses of the beautiful Israel we were flying over. Though we were heading to a battleground, one whose scale I couldn't yet grasp, I couldn't help thinking about the soldiers around me—how, like so many before us, we were about to write the next chapter of Israeli history.

I grew up on stories of Israeli heroism. I remembered the movie about

Yoni Netanyahu, played by Yehoram Gaon in Operation Thunderbolt, in which he led an operation to rescue over a hundred hostages at Entebbe with his Sayeret Matkal troops. I thought of the TV series *Valley of Tears,* when soldiers in the Golan Heights responded to the Yom Kippur War in 1973, fighting against all odds. And I recalled reading about the Six-Day War, when paratroopers like myself reclaimed the Old City of Jerusalem and the Kotel (Western Wall) for the first time in two thousand years. *Har Ha'bayit B'yadeynu*—"The Temple Mount is in our hands."

Sitting in that helicopter, uniform on and gun by my side, I couldn't help but imagine myself in a movie of my own. I didn't know what was to come, only that there was an emergency in the south, and we had been called to the scene.

For the duration of the flight, I kept my eyes focused on the surrounding landscape. After a brief stretch over the Judean desert, a city came into view in the distance. Below us, I spotted the Chords Bridge, the massive white, harp-shaped structure marking the entrance to the holy city of Jerusalem. At that moment, I knew exactly where I was. I looked further into the distance and made out the Old City of Jerusalem, with the iconic Dome of the Rock gleaming at its center. I couldn't believe it. I was heading to a battle zone, flying right over the Capital City.

We passed over Jerusalem and left it behind, continuing toward the Gaza Envelope. My curiosity was sharper than ever, savoring this aerial tour of Israel. But as we approached the Gaza Envelope, the mood shifted. My thoughts snapped back to reality, and I refocused on the mission ahead.

Up at the cockpit of the chopper, the pilot started to notice something unusual. Since I was in the back, I only learned these details later, from an interview done with the pilot. The original plan was to land in an open field adjacent to the Nahal Oz Kibbutz. Both the community and the nearby base had been overrun by terrorists, turning it into one of the major hotspots of October 7th.

As the pilot focused on the ground below, he saw an unsettling movement of people. Knowing that Israeli civilians had been instructed to shelter in their safe rooms, he quickly realized these weren't Israelis. These were terrorists. The figures moving through the area, deep within Israeli territory, were the very ones responsible for this unfolding nightmare.

Landing a helicopter right next to terrorists was out of the question. At the last moment, the pilot made the decision to shift the landing site farther from the border. Southeast of Nahal Oz sits Kibbutz Alumim. Running alongside it was Route 232, an epicenter of the October 7th tragedy, as both Kibbutz Be'eri and the Nova Festival site reside on Route 232 farther south. Across the road from Alumim was an open field—a new target for our landing.

Inside the fuselage of the aircraft, I sat tightly packed with fifty other paratroopers, each of us ready and waiting for our instructions. Standing near the back of the chopper were several members of the helicopter crew, their attention split between us and their communication devices as they relayed updates to the cockpit, and vice versa.

The roar of the helicopter was immense, making even the simplest communication a challenge. Talking was nearly impossible; we relied instead on reading lips, using hand signals, or resorting to a makeshift game of telephone. One person would lean in and scream a message into someone's ear, who would then pass it on by yelling into the next guy's ear.

At a certain point, one of the helicopter crew members—the one responsible for giving us instructions—told us to stand up and prepare for departure. Through the chaotic game of telephone, we learned that we were landing in just a few moments. Since we were entering an active combat zone, the helicopter needed to land, unload all the soldiers, and leave the area as quickly as possible. At the time, we had no idea that the pilot had spotted terrorists below, nor were we aware of the full extent of the situation in Israel.

We all stood up, and the benches lining both sides of the helicopter folded neatly against the walls. With our guns slung around our necks, our bags at our feet, and our hands gripping the handles scattered throughout the cabin, we braced ourselves for landing. And then we waited.

Standing on my feet gave me a clearer view of the outside. I turned my head to peek through a window and then—BOOM!

The helicopter jolted violently. We lost our footing and crashed to the floor as if struck by an earthquake. But that wasn't what this was. We'd been hit by a Hamas rocket.

INTRODUCTION

"Come in, welcome. *Shabbat Shalom!* Can I take your coat?"

You step through the door and are immediately greeted by the unmistakable smell of Shabbat dinner. Chicken, potatoes, salad, vegetables, rice—and there on the counter sits a parve chocolate babka, but you'll have to wait until the end for that treat. You've made it to the right place.

But it's the smell from the oven that truly draws you in. That warm, golden challah is nearly ready. The classic Jewish bread eaten every Friday night—braided, fluffy, slightly sweet, and always delicious. Just this morning, it was a lump of dough. My mom took yeast, flour, and all the secret ingredients, kneaded it with care, let it rise, braided it, and placed it in the oven. Now, it's no longer dough—it's bread. That smell, that challah smell, goes straight to your soul.

"Come, sit down, take a seat."

You settle onto the couch. "*Shabbat Shalom!* Thank you for coming." All that food on the counter and in the oven—we'll wait just a little longer, at least until Shabbat officially begins. Soon we'll light the candles, bless the wine, wash our hands, make the blessing on the challah, and then we'll dive into the meal. And yes, only after the meal will that warm babka make its way to your plate. Patience.

But this isn't just any Shabbat dinner.

"Welcome home," you say. From where? We'll get to that. "Welcome home…where do I even begin?" And truly, where does one begin?

Let me take a step back. My name is Ira Mitchell Kohler. You can call me Ira—or Nisi, my Hebrew name. My parents named me Nisi Melech Kohler in Hebrew. *Nisi* means "my miracle," and *Melech* means "king." So yes, I suppose that makes me a king. A king of what, exactly? Good question. That's why I usually stick with Ira, whether I'm in America or Israel.

For five months, I was in the middle of a massive war. On October 7, 2023, Hamas attacked Israel. I was rushed to the Gaza Envelope and fought on the front lines that very day. A few weeks later, I entered Gaza itself and fought there for over a hundred days, deep in enemy territory.

Now I'm home—thank G-d—and sitting here across from you. But who are *you*?

You could be anyone. Maybe we've shared many Shabbat dinners before. Maybe we're close friends, but it's the first time you're at my house. Maybe we've met briefly, shared only a few words. Maybe we've never met at all. Maybe you've heard of me. Or I've heard of you. Maybe you're a complete stranger and, truthfully, I'm wondering how you got in here. Just kidding. You can stay.

But there's something obvious, something lingering in the room. I just came home from war. I served as a Lone Soldier in the 890th Battalion of the IDF Paratroopers. A Lone Soldier is someone serving in the Israel Defense Forces (IDF) without immediate family or familial support in Israel. My parents live in New York, so I was considered a Lone Soldier. Now, sitting here with you, it's clear you've got questions. But where do you begin?

You want to ask about Gaza. But how do you ask about an experience that spanned over one hundred days? How do you bring up Gaza without starting with October 7th? Where was I that day? What happened? And even before that—what brought me to the IDF in the first place? I'm not Israeli, or am I? You want to know what my life was like before the army. So much to ask. Where do you start?

Suddenly, Shabbat dinner feels like a Passover seder, staying up all night retelling the story—only this time, it's not about Egypt but Gaza. Let's be real, though: You leave by 11:00 p.m., a respectable hour. We touched on a few things. You asked a couple of questions. I answered what I could. There were meaningful moments. But how deep did we go? A dent in the surface would be generous.

This was a Shabbat dinner, after all—my family, you, and a few others. The night wasn't going to revolve around me, and I wouldn't have allowed it anyway. We talked about you, what's going on in town, and yes, the usual politics. Maybe you hoped to leave with a full picture of my time in the war, but that was never going to happen over one meal.

It's not because I'm unwilling to talk or too shaken to share. The truth is: It's hard. Five months of war can't be condensed into one dinner conversation. I aged a lifetime then. Organizing all of it—my stories, thoughts, emotions—into something coherent? I'm not sure I can do that in a book. But I can try.

I'm a New Yorker through and through. I am a huge sports fan—especially football. Go Giants! I was raised with a strong Jewish identity, and at twenty-one, I moved to Israel with one goal: to serve in the IDF. I enlisted in January 2022. With less than three months left in my service, I was dreaming of a trip to Thailand, the place many soldiers go after their service ends. But Hamas had other plans. They sent me to Gaza. Sort of. Actually, they probably didn't want me in Gaza—but hey, they started the war.

I fought for five months in what will be remembered as one of Israel's toughest wars. And now, to my mother's great relief, I'm back home—sitting at our dining room table on Long Island. You, my guest, are here with me. There's a lot to talk about. So where do we begin?

We begin with this book. Take some chicken. Pass the challah. Let's get to it! And next time? Shabbat dinner at your place. I'll bring the babka.

Now that you understand the main reason for this book, let me clarify a few things. This isn't a history book or an analysis of the Middle East. There will be some history, and we'll discuss the Middle East because, well, Israel is in the Middle East, and context matters. But that's not the focus.

I'm here to share my story. The story of how I, a nice Jewish boy from Long Island, crossed the ocean, enlisted in the IDF, and fought on the front lines during one of the worst terrorist attacks in history, followed by the war that ensued.

This is a story of what it's like to be a soldier, especially during the toughest moments. It's also a story that aims to offer some clarity—some understanding—of what life was truly like for a soldier in the war, particularly while fighting in Gaza.

Jewish tradition has a unique way of preserving the past. We don't simply recount history—we tell stories. Our collective story includes Passover, the daring escape from Egypt where the Israelites fled bondage under Pharaoh and, with the aid of miracles, made their way to a land flowing with milk and honey—or today, hummus and tehina.

In every generation, through triumph and tragedy, more stories are born and shared. Growing up, I heard Holocaust survivors recount their experiences. Each survivor's story was unique—a personal timeline, perspective, and choice of details. Even siblings who endured the Holocaust together could tell their stories differently. The general themes might align, but their individual perspectives and memories created distinct narratives.

This brings me to the point: What you're about to read is my story. It's not a comprehensive history of the events or a complete account of every moment in this complex war. It's my personal experience—what I saw, felt, and pieced together over time.

After October 7th, I often spoke with my friends in the army—the same friends who fought alongside me. As we recounted the fighting in Kibbutz Be'eri, we noticed that while our stories shared similarities, they also differed in many ways.

Why? Because perspective matters. If I'm standing next to a friend, less than a meter apart, with my gun raised, and he's looking right while I'm looking left, we see different things. We're in the same place at the same time, but our experiences differ. Similarly, during an operation in Gaza, when we uncovered a stockpile of Hamas rockets, I was at the front while my friend was behind me. We shared the mission and the success, but what stood out to each of us was different.

This illustrates a larger idea about how wars—and this Israel–Hamas war in particular—will be remembered and taught. How will we explain what happened? How will we convey what we experienced? The answer is simple: through the stories we tell. And since this is my story, based on what I saw and lived, it won't be something you can fact-check. Like any story, you can choose to believe it or not.

Welcome to my story—the transformation of an American becoming a dual American–Israeli citizen, serving in Israel's war of all wars.

CHAPTER 1

MY STORY BEGINS

Gaza Border, February 28, 2024

Heading back into Israel, I watched as we approached the border fence and as that fence became a sight in our rearview mirrors. The war, life in Gaza, and everything I had learned over the past hundred days was now a thing of yesterday. Ahead lay not only a beautiful country, one filled with a Jewish spirit, an innovative mind, and delicious shawarma, but also my entire life. Ahead stood freedom, opportunity, and fear. Not only was this another successful mission, but for me it meant the end of my service. I was leaving the army. The thought hit me, but I didn't yet know how to feel about it.

Our vehicle stopped at an open field near the border. A massive tent had been set up where we would spend the night before heading to our base. The mood was electric. There was a barbeque where American volunteers were grilling up the best of the best: chicken, steak, and, yes, more steak. Music played and everyone was dancing. There were smiles, laughter, pictures taken, and good vibes all around.

We had just left Gaza after four months of deployment. Our

battalion, the 890th Battalion of the Paratrooper Brigade, was scheduled to have a long break, and there was no indication we were returning to Gaza anytime soon. For me, however, this moment meant something different. I enlisted in the IDF on January 4, 2022, signing up for a two-year service. Due to the war, I decided to stay a bit longer in the reserves, or as the Israelis call it, as a *miluimnik*. With our time in Gaza coming to an end, I knew my service was coming to an end. This was the time, as I promised everyone, especially my mother, that I was going to turn in my gun and call my service complete. I had done enough, more than I was expected to, and the time was right.

I grabbed some food, stood off to the side next to my friend, and looked around. I watched a battalion full of soldiers smiling, partying it up. And, kudos to them. Kudos to us! After four months in Gaza, some steak and dancing was not only uplifting but well deserved. As I stood there, that's when it hit me. This was really happening. My service was coming to an end.

Several emotions hit me. I was scared—scared of what lay in the world ahead. I didn't know what my next steps would be, and after several years within the structure and routine of the IDF, the lack of a plan was surely frightening.

I felt a bit sad. As strange as it sounds, I knew I would miss this. Not the discomfort, not the danger—but the meaning. The purpose. Fighting alongside friends, risking everything for something bigger than ourselves—that gave life a clarity nothing else ever had. Watching everyone laugh and celebrate only reminded me how deeply I'd come to value it all.

I also felt guilty, unaccomplished. I had promised myself I wouldn't finish my service until Omer came home. Omer Neutra, my childhood friend, was one of the hostages taken during October 7th. From the moment I learned he was taken, I carried that with me—every operation, every night in Gaza. And now here I was, finishing my service while he was still in captivity. I promised myself that as long as he was underground in Hamas's tunnels, I would be in Gaza fighting for his return. This promise I made to myself was one I was breaking. This was the right moment to finish my service, and I knew, deep down, that I couldn't wait. Who knew how long it would take, or if Omer would ever come home?

After a round of steak, I obviously went for seconds. After that, for thirds. Who am I kidding? I love steak. That night we slept outside in a big white tent right near the Gaza border. Laying down, I wondered what came next. Where would I go from here? I didn't know where I'd go, where I'd work, or how I'd pass my days.

For five months, carrying a gun gave me a real, tangible, and effective way to fight. I was on the front lines. I had understood that, appreciated that, and showed up when our people needed it most. However, that gun, I realized, gave me a voice to tell my story. Being on the front lines, people respected and really listened to what I had to say. I was their first source, their closest connection to what was happening. With this voice, there was a new purpose. I shared my story and spoke to communities of all kinds. From synagogues to schools, youth groups to college campuses, I shared my experiences from the war.

And that gun gave me not only a voice to speak but also a voice to write, to write about who I am, where I came from, everything I went through, and my emotions, challenges, and triumphs throughout the war.

So, as I sat down to write, I knew I had to go back, all the way to the beginning. Because this story isn't just about the missions in Gaza or the movie-like scenes of October 7th. It's about identity, belief, sacrifice, and the values instilled in me from a young age.

You might think my story begins in Gaza, inside a school and across from a hospital—which was actually a Hamas base—but my story starts in Queens, New York, where I was born, followed four minutes later by my twin brother, Jeremy. Though he may not be quite as good-looking as me, he's done all right. Together, we were the first two children of Michael and Beth.

We lived in a small apartment in Great Neck, New York, for the first three years of our lives. But with another baby on the way, my family needed an upgrade. A month before my sister, Shira, was born, we moved into the house in Plainview, New York, where I grew up.

Family was central to my upbringing. On my mom's side, I am surrounded by six aunts and uncles, nine cousins, and two grandparents. My dad's side is a bit smaller, with three aunts and uncles, two cousins, and my grandmother. Sadly, my grandfather, Larry Kohler, *Z"L*, passed away the summer after I graduated from high school.

As a child, I was a good kid but a bit wild. I had no fear, which explains the many times I needed stitches or staples in my head. This crazy energy naturally brought me to sports, and I played just about everything: soccer, basketball, baseball, tennis, floor hockey, and ultimate Frisbee. Watching sports became a passion too. I'm a big fan of the Mets, Islanders, Knicks, and Giants. Fall Sundays spent watching football became a weekly staple. If that's not American, I don't know what is.

But the most defining part of my childhood was my connection to Judaism, Israel, and the Jewish community at large. My parents sent my siblings and me to the Schechter School of Long Island, a private Jewish day school, from kindergarten through twelfth grade. At Schechter, I learned about Israel, the Jewish holidays, Hebrew, and texts from the Tanach and Talmud. Jewish education became an integral component of my upbringing. My family was also deeply involved in our synagogue, Midway Jewish Center. We attended services on Shabbat and holidays, and it was where my siblings and I were called to the Torah as a Bar Mitzvah. My dad even served as synagogue president, and my brother and I each served as presidents for the synagogue's youth group.

Summers were for camp. My parents sent us to the Young Judaea camps at Sprout Lake when we were younger and Tel Yehudah in high school. These camps became a home away from home, and there was no better place for me to grow and mature. They offered a chance to unplug, have fun with friends, and gain independence, all while living and breathing Judaism and Israel 24/7. Young Judaea, being a Zionist youth movement, ensured that Israel, its culture, and its people were always at the forefront of our experiences. I loved it so much that I returned as a counselor and, later, as a unit head, or *merekez*. To this day I love visiting camp; it feels like going home.

My childhood centered around Israel in more ways than I realized at the time. Our family, being active members of the Long Island Jewish community, hosted several *shinshinim* through the Jewish Agency. *Shinshinim* are Israelis who spend a year abroad between high school and their military service. These young Israelis come to communities worldwide to volunteer, teach, and show what Israel is like. Each *shinshin* needs a host family, and mine decided to be the first during the program's pilot year. Over the next six years we hosted four different *shinshinim*, all close to my age.

Beyond bringing Israel home to Long Island, we also brought ourselves to this tiny sliver of a nation in the Middle East. I was six years old when I first visited Israel, and over the course of my childhood, I returned several more times. These visits took Israel off a screen and away from the pages of a book and showed me the breath, soul, and, of course, the food of our homeland.

This environment I was raised in laid the foundation for my love of Israel and Judaism. When I decided to enlist in the IDF, later, I didn't have a singular "aha" moment or spiritual awakening—it was simply the fabric of my upbringing.

After high school, I faced the big decision of where to go to college. While I considered taking a gap year in Israel, a decision both my sister and brother made, I ultimately decided to head straight to the University of Delaware.

The experiences and choices I made during my time at Delaware set the stage for my decision to serve in the IDF. Over the years, my perspective drifted further from a typical American path, moving instead toward fulfilling my dream of serving the Jewish State.

In August 2018, I drove down the Jersey Turnpike from my home on Long Island, crossed the Delaware Memorial Bridge, and arrived at the University of Delaware—the place I would call home for the next few years. I was both excited and nervous. Moving from a small Jewish day school with a graduating class of thirty-seven to a university with a freshman class of over five thousand was intimidating, to say the least. My dorm alone was more than three times the size of my entire high school.

I arrived on campus with my mom, dad, brother, and sister. We unpacked my many bags into my new freshman dorm room. I didn't bring any decorations, so my dad suggested hanging my Jacob deGrom Mets jersey and my Eli Manning Giants jersey by my bed. It was a simple yet efficient way to bring some color to the room—and it turned out to be a pretty common theme among the guys on my floor. The girls' dorms were always more thoughtfully decorated, but at least I put in some effort.

I worried about college. Would I like it? Would I make friends? Would I fit in? I wasn't an outgoing or particularly social person, and the thought of being a small fish in such a big sea was daunting. But I knew I had to take the plunge. After unpacking, I told my family, "I'm good to go from here." I said goodbye and took my first steps into my college years.

In those first few weeks, I pushed myself out of my comfort zone. I met people in my dorm, through Hillel and Chabad on campus, and in my classes. Joining the ultimate Frisbee team with a friend from my dorm turned out to be one of the best decisions I made. I started building friendships that, I hope, will last a lifetime.

College was fun. With only a few hours of class and studying each day, I had plenty of time to hang out with friends, explore new interests, and enjoy myself. I spent a lot of time at Hillel, the Jewish center on campus, and Frisbee practices became a regular part of my routine. The schoolwork wasn't too hard, and even when it was, the enjoyable college lifestyle made up for it.

But something was missing. While I enjoyed college, I struggled to connect with the Jewish community in the same way I had at home. Jewish life on campus was different. For one thing, there were no Shabbat morning services.

As my second semester began, a thought started to take shape. I couldn't tell you exactly why or how, but I began considering enlisting in the IDF. It wasn't a new idea—I'd thought about it before—but this time, it felt different. I started researching online, watching videos of Lone Soldiers, and learning everything I could about serving in the IDF.

Enlisting in a foreign military, no matter how much of a connection one has to that country, isn't the normal path one takes in life. Usually, after one gets their bachelor's degree, they look for a job or pursue further education. Clearly, that wasn't me. In my final semester at the University of Delaware, seniors received a "what-are-you-doing-next-year" survey, with about ten different choices, none of which included "other." There was an option for enlisting in the American military, but surprise-surprise, making *aliyah* and enlisting in the IDF wasn't there. Among all the seniors that year, let's just say I was different.

The question of "why" always comes up. Why put oneself through the hardships of an IDF service? For what purpose? The answer to these questions requires me to take a step back, to explain ever so slightly how I feel about Israel and my love and connection to the Jewish people.

We're so lucky to be living in a time when Israel exists. For two thousand years, the Jewish people prayed for a return to our homeland. Every Passover seder we say, *"L'shana ha'baah b'yerushalayim,"* which means "Next year in Jerusalem." We continue saying prayers about our land because we know that as Jews, we feel a strong connection between a people, our G-d, and our homeland. Exiled from our home and without Jewish sovereignty in the Land of Israel, a part of our peoplehood was missing.

Now, after two thousand years, we can finally say we have a home. On the world stage, the Jewish people are represented and mean something. We have representation in the United Nations and other global bodies, and we have ambassadors throughout the world. If, G-d forbid, another Holocaust is to happen, the Jewish people have a place to go. With the State of Israel, Jews are no longer seen as weak but rather strong, willing to fight back and survive. Our Hebrew language has been revived, and we now can read ancient scripts, as well as order coffee, in our own language. A new Israeli culture has been born. We can walk where our ancestors walked, and the land that G-d promised us is now ours. It's our home. How lucky are we?

A return to Israel wasn't going to come in the form of kings like David, or in a mighty empire. A return to Israel, and a return to the Jewish homeland, would mean establishing a nation state for the Jewish people in our ancestral homeland. The modern State of Israel, established on May 14, 1948, was that dream come true. Israelis danced in the street as finally, after a long wait, our time had come. The next day, however, showed Israelis the responsibility of keeping that dream alive. With several surrounding countries all attacking Israel on May 15, trying to annihilate the newly established State of Israel, the Jewish people had to flip the switch. We were no longer the Jews of Europe, sent to concentration camps, but rather a new Jew, strong and ready to fight back against invading forces.

In the War of Independence, six thousand men and women were lost in the fight to protect Israel; to put it more strikingly, Israel lost one percent of its population. For a country so small, the loss was devastating. However, Israel survived and thrived.

From that moment on, Israelis had a responsibility. If we had dreamed of a Jewish State for two thousand years, and on May 14, 1948, that dream came true, then every day afterward we have a modern-day responsibility to keep that dream alive, to keep Israel safe and breathing.

While there are exceptions, both men and women in Israel are required to serve in the IDF. Whether they serve in the most elite special forces units or in a much less physically demanding role, taking a few years between high school and the "real world" to serve our country is how we ensure Israel continues to exist for generations to come.

When I am asked the "why" question, oftentimes people expect an "aha" moment. As if there was a moment when I had some sort of divine realization that this—serving in the IDF—was what I had to do, as if something was calling me to do it. The truth was nothing close to that. I was raised in a community where Judaism and Israel weren't part of who we are, but rather the essence of who we are. A community where visiting the holy land and staying up-to-date on Israeli current events wasn't an exception but the norm.

As I left my Jewish bubble after high school and started my college years, for the first time I encountered a world that was different from the one I'd known before. My appreciation of Judaism and Israel only grew stronger. It was hard sitting in Business 101 while other eighteen-year-olds were learning how to shoot a rifle. I felt a real sense of responsibility to protect Israel. How lucky I was to be living in a time when Israel exists. I knew that Israel was a country not only for Israeli citizens but for Jews worldwide. With that love of Israel and deep sense of responsibility, I wanted to be part of keeping the country alive for generations to come.

In late February of my freshman year, I finally worked up the courage to tell my parents. When I called, they were in shock and didn't know what to say. It wasn't until the next day that they could fully express their feelings. They supported me and understood where I was coming from, but they weren't thrilled about the idea. My mom, especially, was scared. No parent wants to send their child to the military, let alone a combat unit in another country. They encouraged me to finish my degree first, hoping that, with time, I might change my mind.

I wasn't going to let that happen. The thought of waiting four years was unbearable, so I made the decision to accelerate my studies and graduate in three years instead of four. With many credits already under my belt, I declared a major in economics and added minors in education and Jewish studies. Since I was putting my career on hold, I felt it was essential to create a well-rounded academic experience that would provide me with diverse options after completing my service.

I also prepared for my future in Israel. I worked out, studied Hebrew, and read everything I could about Israel's history, culture, and military. During the COVID-19 pandemic, I developed a habit of reading about Israel and ended up finishing over thirty books on the topic. These efforts gave me the clarity and motivation I needed.

In the spring of 2020, I prepared to spend a semester abroad at the Hebrew University of Jerusalem through the Nachshon Project.

Unfortunately, COVID-19 cut the semester short, but it only strengthened my resolve. I returned home, finished my degree, and graduated at the top of my class—a whole year early.

Leaving college and my friends early was tough, but I knew the timing was crucial. The further I moved from the age of eighteen, the harder it would be to pick up and move to Israel, serve in the IDF, and fulfill my dream. With my degree in hand and my preparations complete, I was ready to take the next step.

CHAPTER 2

MOVING TO ISRAEL

Aliyah Date, August 18, 2021

The moment it all felt real happened a few months before my *aliyah* date. One of my friends had made the move before me and watching him take that step hit me hard. He flew to Israel on an *aliyah* charter flight, where every single passenger onboard was heading to Israel for the same purpose—a one-way ticket to immigrate, to make *aliyah*. When he arrived at Ben Gurion Airport, the celebration was unforgettable. Crowds of Israelis gathered to greet the new arrivals. They held signs from Nefesh B'Nefesh, the organization that assists Jews making *aliyah*, and sang Israeli songs filled with hope and pride.

I watched the event unfold on a Facebook live stream, and my heart raced with excitement. My moment was coming, and soon enough, I'd be in that same place.

I moved to Israel through a program called Garin Tzabar. The word *garin* means "seed" or "nucleus," and *tzabar* refers to the sabra fruit—tough and prickly on the outside, soft and sweet on the inside. It's often used to describe Israelis and their unique blend of resilience and warmth.

The program is designed to help young Jews from around the world acclimate to life in Israel and prepare for service in the IDF.

Each year, hundreds of aspiring immigrants join Garin Tzabar and are divided into small groups, called *garinim*. My group later became known as Garin Rimonim, which translates to "Pomegranate Group." The name wasn't just random—outside the clubhouse of our kibbutz, pomegranate trees grew abundantly. We had a habit of picking the fruit, peeling the seeds, and snacking on them during our activities. It became a part of our identity. The other name in contention was "Sea Turtles," so you can guess why we went with pomegranates.

There were seventeen of us in Garin Rimonim, all from North America, all sharing the dream of serving in the IDF. Garin Tzabar placed us at Kibbutz Erez, but before we moved, we spent six months meeting as a group in North America. This was during the height of the COVID-19 pandemic, so all our meetings were virtual. From January to June 2021, we gathered on Zoom to discuss the challenges ahead—*aliyah*, the IDF, Israeli culture, and, most importantly, why we were doing this.

When one of our members made *aliyah* in April, the idea that we were all about to leave our former lives behind became real. While others in my garin moved at staggered times, I waited until August 2021. The program didn't officially begin until then, and I still had college to finish. After earning my degree, I spent the summer working at my sleepaway camp, Sprout Lake. Saying goodbye to my family and friends was difficult, knowing I wouldn't see them again for at least eighteen months.

On August 17, 2021, the day finally arrived. With my parents, brother, and sister by my side, I made my way to JFK International Airport. After the typical security checks with El Al staff, I walked to the gate, boarded the plane, and that was it, no turning back.

The flight landed with the usual chaos of a flight to Israel—applause, scattered cheers, and the Olympic sprint to stand in the aisle, only to wait bumper-to-bumper for the doors to open. Nothing out of the ordinary.

It was noon on Wednesday, August 18, when my plane finally touched down in Israel. I stepped off and began weaving my way through Ben Gurion Airport, surrounded by fellow *olim* (new immigrants to Israel)—all of us slightly dazed, slightly sweaty, and very much aware that life was about to change.

We stopped at designated points to receive our *teudat oleh* (new immigrant card) and other papers that would soon become our golden tickets—or bureaucratic burdens—for getting an Israeli ID (*teudat zehut*), opening a bank account, and more. We dealt with customs, retrieved our luggage, and got a friendly COVID-19 swab up the nose.

But Ben Gurion Airport isn't really Israel. It's a sterile, air-conditioned bubble, a holding pen between the life you just left and the one you're about to enter. It wasn't until I stepped outside, toward the sign reading "New Olim," and climbed into the free Nefesh B'Nefesh taxi, that I felt like I was truly starting this new chapter of my life.

The driver was exactly who you'd imagine: tan skin, deep voice, one hand on the wheel, the other holding a cigarette between two fingers. The windows were down, Mizrachi-Israeli music was playing from the radio, and the Tel Aviv skyline was passing by on the right. He knew I was an *oleh* (immigrant) and asked where I was heading, then said nothing else.

We drove in silence. I stared out the window, drinking in this strange, sun-drenched land. Ten hours on a plane and a years-long journey before that—all culminating in this moment, in this cab, with this man and his cigarette.

Then, suddenly, he broke the silence. "There is one thing you need to know," he said.

I sat up a little straighter. My first piece of advice in my new country.

A meaningful insight? A cultural tip? A warm welcome? I was ready.

He continued, in Hebrew-accented English: "When you leave your quarantine place, leave your phone at home. The government will track you."

That was it. No elaboration. Just that. We returned to silence.

I wanted to laugh. I mean—of course. My first "pro tip" as an Israeli citizen was a loophole for dodging quarantine enforcement. Not exactly the Zionist inspiration I had imagined. But maybe it *was* a kind of wisdom. Maybe this was less about rules and more about attitude. About how Israelis look at life: independently, skeptically, always one step ahead of the system.

I smiled and leaned back in my seat. *Welcome to Israel*, I thought. *Welcome to Israel.*

I moved to Kibbutz Erez, the place I would call home for the next two years. It was where I spent my breaks from the army and found a community to which I would form a deep attachment. Erez is beautiful, peaceful, warm, and full of life. I loved wandering through its neighborhoods, passing the cows, picking fruit straight from the trees, and hiking up the hill to catch a sunset view with Gaza in the distance.

Each summer, the kibbutz came alive when the pool opened. On weekends, it felt like the whole community gathered there to relax. Erez had it all: a clubhouse, a dining hall, a mini market, a pub, and the beloved Oryoss Café. That spot was more than just a local hangout—it drew people from all over Israel. On Saturdays, the lawn outside the café would fill with visitors enjoying fresh pastries and coffee in the sun. The kibbutz also housed a plastic factory and its own honey factory, producing rich, sweet honey you could only get right there in Erez.

The best part of Kibbutz Erez, though, was the people. And one of the greatest things about Garin Tzabar was our host families, who were there to support us in various ways. I was matched with a wonderful family—Eli and Geula, who had two young children, Noa and Omer. They were ages six and two when I first met them in 2021, and by now, they've certainly grown quite a bit! I spent many holidays and Shabbat dinners with them, and they helped me with anything I needed throughout my service. They were my connection to the greater kibbutz community, and I'll always be grateful for their support, especially during the war. Kibbutz Erez gave me a home, a family, and a support system that would always be there for me.

Kibbutz Erez sits just eight hundred meters from the Gaza border, which when I first moved there was described to me as "a slice of paradise minutes from hell." Locals often say, *"Ein li Erez acheret,"* or "I have no other Erez." It's a twist on the famous 1986 song "Ein Li Eretz Acheret" ("I Have No Other Country") by Gali Atari—a phrase that's taken on new weight since October 7th. For many Israelis, there truly is no other country; for the people of Erez, there's no other home. And when they say it, they mean it.

A kibbutz isn't like a typical town—it's a close-knit community built on shared responsibility, originally rooted in socialism. Everyone worked for the kibbutz, and the kibbutz supported everyone in return. Though most have since moved away from that model, the spirit of unity remains strong. In times of tragedy or joy, the whole community feels it together. There was no tragedy that hit Kibbutz Erez harder than the tragedy of October 7th, one that affected an entire country and an entire people worldwide.

Fortunately, while other neighboring kibbutzim dealt with widespread massacres, the heroism in Erez saved the community. Only one member of Erez was killed in the kibbutz that day. But, as I mentioned, when tragedy strikes one, it strikes all. The whole community felt the loss of Amir Naim, may his memory be a blessing. Amir served in the Yahalom unit of the IDF. He was in the middle of his college studies and married his wife on October 1, 2022, a year before his death. Before starting his studies in 2021, Amir agreed to be our *madrich* (counselor) in Garin Tzabar, leading trips and discussions about Israel and the IDF.

Amir always spoke about his experiences in the military, specifically, stories of his time as a combat soldier. He would joke about how "stupid" we Americans were for leaving the US to enlist in the IDF, but he understood the importance of serving. He was always supportive.

In addition to his studies, Amir served on the Kibbutz Erez security team, or *kitah konenuit*. Many communities in Israel, especially those near Gaza, have their own security teams, which act as the first responders before the police, army, or any other security forces arrive. On October 7, 2023, around thirty terrorists attacked Kibbutz Erez. Amir and the security team, with help from the neighboring community of Or Ha'Ner, managed to fight off every last terrorist, saving the kibbutz. Unlike many other communities along the Gaza border, no terrorists managed to enter Erez, and the damage was minimal. Erez was saved.

Despite the heroism of the security team, Amir lost his life in the battle. He sacrificed his life to save the community. Amir leaves behind his wife and his newborn baby, born half a year after his death.

His funeral took place about a week and a half after October 7th in Rishon Le'tzion, as no one was allowed to return to Erez at that time. But a year later, on October 8, 2024, Amir's body was finally moved back to Kibbutz Erez and laid to rest in the community he had fought so hard to protect. The entire kibbutz came together to honor him. At last, Amir was back where he belonged.

Since then, most of the kibbutz families have returned to their homes. After being displaced to Mitzpe Ramon and then Kiryat Gat for nearly a year, many families came back in time for the new school year in September 2024. They're slowly rebuilding their lives and trying to move forward after everything they've been through.

Kibbutz Erez is beautiful. It's a community built on love, family, and belonging. It was my home throughout my IDF service, and I owe it so much. It was struck by tragedy but saved by its people, and now, as it tries to heal, it's a community still holding onto the memory of Amir's sacrifice. Above all, Kibbutz Erez is defined by its community, and I'm proud to have been part of it.

When I moved to Israel, I couldn't have told you how much this home would mean to me. I felt lucky not only moving to Israel and serving in the IDF but also finding a home in Erez. My host family, the Garin Tzabar family, and the wider Erez community became an integral part of my time in Israel, and as I began my military service, this home became a place of comfort during my breaks away from base.

CHAPTER 3

IDF SERVICE BEFORE OCTOBER 7TH

Paratrooper Training Base, February 16, 2022

At around 4:30 in the afternoon, we were split into our groups. I was at *gibbush tzanhanim*, the official tryout to see if I had what it takes to be a paratrooper. This tryout was our test, and only those who passed would be accepted into the unit.

The main physical portion of the tryout was about to start. We arrived at a large, flat, sandy area. We stretched, warmed up, loosened our bodies, and prepared ourselves for what was coming.

"On the line."

Twenty-five of us lined up shoulder to shoulder on a line that barely fit fifteen. We squeezed in, jostling for space, each of us trying to push an elbow in front of the guy next to us for just a bit of running room. The main judge placed a cone twenty to twenty-five meters away and gave us our instruction: "The goal is to run around the cone from this side and come back to the starting line."

"*Tzuh ha'derech!*"—"Go!"

We took off, sprinting toward the cone, looping around it, and racing back. When we returned, the judge explained the system: The first five to make it back stood in front of one cone; the last five stood behind another. Only the names of the top five and bottom five were recorded.

Now the pressure was on.

I wasn't too worried about ending up in the bottom five—I consistently ran in the top third of the group—but getting sixth or seventh felt like a wasted effort. If I was going to push, I needed to be in the top five. Still, I knew I couldn't go all-out every single round, or I'd burn out too fast. Every sprint I decided how much effort I'd give based on how tired I felt, where I stood on the line, and whether I had a real shot of making it into the top five.

"Tzuh ha'derech!"

Sometimes I sprinted hard and made it into the top five. Other times, I held back a bit and recovered some energy. Then the judge raised the stakes—only the top three would be recorded from now on. The competition became even tighter. When I knew I was close, I flung my body forward at the finish line like a Frisbee player making a diving layout catch. Sometimes it worked, and I landed in the top three. Sometimes I came up short. Still, I hoped the judges saw the effort.

We must have done about fifteen of those sprints before moving on. And that was just the beginning.

Next came crawling exercises. We dragged ourselves back and forth across the sand to see who could push through and who would tap out. I moved like a snake, flinging myself forward with everything I had. Sand got into my clothes, my eyes, my mouth. I ignored it all and kept crawling.

Then came another round of sprinting, this time with the *alunka*— the stretcher. After each sprint the first four people to reach the stretcher had to grab the handles, lift the stretcher in the air, and carry it through the next sprint. Only those carrying it were noted. Out of the eight or nine rounds, I made it to the stretcher three times—not bad in a group of twenty-five. I dove for those handles more than once, sometimes making it, sometimes just missing. Once, I was neck and neck with someone else and launched myself forward, grabbing the stretcher by sheer instinct. That time, I got it.

We did other drills as well, such as push-ups and planks without knowing when they'd end. That was part of the test: Could you endure when there was no clear finish line? They also threw in a few team-building and public speaking exercises, likely to evaluate our social skills and leadership under pressure.

At the very end, we faced the toughest exercise of the day. They combined crawling, sprinting, and sandbag work into one brutal, continuous drill. We started by crawling to a line about two-thirds of the way across the field. Then we had to stand up, lift a heavy sandbag over our heads, sprint to the end line, turn around, come back to where we picked it up, drop it, and sprint back to the starting line. After finishing, we had to scream, *"Echad!"*—"One!"

Then we did it again. This time, *"Shtayim!"*—"Two!"

And again. Over and over. Every round, the number increased. It became a test of mental grit more than physical strength.

This is where I truly shone.

Early in the drill, I got stuck behind a few slower crawlers and fell behind. But once I got out of that bottleneck, I surged ahead. I began leading the pack, yelling the next number before most others finished the previous round. When I screamed *"Tesha!"*—"Nine!"—others were still on seven or eight. In the end, I hit thirteen rounds. Only a couple of others reached twelve. Most hovered around nine or ten. I was proud, as this was the final sprint of the fourth quarter, and I gave it everything I had.

When we finally stopped, the main judge congratulated us. He said we gave it our all, and he was right. I had never physically pushed myself like that before. I threw my body around recklessly, acting on raw instinct. That night I felt completely wrecked, and four days later, my upper body was still sore from all the crawling.

Three weeks after the *gibbush*, I finally received my official acceptance. I would be a paratrooper in the IDF.

✡ ✡ ✡

While most of this book focuses on my experiences in the war, before I delve into that, I need to share a bit about my service prior to October 7th. I enlisted on January 4, 2022, and began my service at Michve Alon, a base for new immigrants to improve their Hebrew before moving into the larger IDF framework. Over three months, the entire focus was on learning Hebrew—a challenging yet vital step.

During my time at Michve Alon, I expressed my desire to serve in a combat unit and requested the paratroopers, one of five main infantry units along with Golani, Givati, Nahal, and Kfir. Unlike these other units, the paratrooper unit required passing a tryout, and my story above is a glimpse into that. To my delight, I was accepted into the unit, and by the end of my Hebrew course, I knew where I'd be serving. We celebrated the conclusion of the Hebrew course with a ceremony at the Kotel (Western Wall) in Jerusalem. After a two-week break, I began my service in the Paratrooper Brigade on April 7, 2022.

That April morning mirrored my enlistment day. But instead of traveling north, I headed south to Bach Tzanhanim, the paratrooper training base, where my true service began. During my first week, I participated in another *gibbush* for the elite units of Maglan, Duvdevan, and the paratrooper special forces battalion. Though I completed the tryout—an achievement in and of itself—I didn't pass. I was instead assigned to the 890th Battalion, one of the three regular battalions in the paratroopers, along with the 101st and 202nd Battalions.

The next eight months were the hardest part of my service. Training was grueling, both physically and mentally. Unlike real combat, training involved relentless discipline, constant correction from our commanders, and punishments for our failures. To make an American reference, IDF training is akin to rushing a fraternity, except those in charge were trained IDF commanders and not crazy college students. Our days were strictly regimented, filled with endless running and rigorous drills. Yet we learned critical skills as well: shooting, fieldwork, parachuting during a two-week course that culminated in three jumps, and how to work and fight as a team. This period concluded with the iconic *masa kumta*—a fifty-kilometer march ending in Jerusalem, where we received our red berets and officially became paratroopers. After this march, we moved into our active service.

Every four months during my active service, our battalion changed its primary "home." We go from four months of *kav* (guarding) to four months of *imun* (training) and then repeat that cycle over and over again. This doesn't mean we don't train during our four months of guarding, or that we don't guard during the four months of training, but generally speaking, we alternate between the two every four months. It's a constant cycle of training and operational duties.

Throughout my service, my battalion's assignments were exclusively in the West Bank, including Karnei Shomron, Homesh, Horesh Yaron, and, most notably, the city of Hebron. In Hebron, we guarded the section of the city between the Jewish communities of Kiriyat Arba and Harsina, and the Jewish section of Hebron itself, which includes the Cave of the Patriarchs (Maarat HaMachpela). I served there for over four months, from late February to early July 2023.

After Hebron, my battalion moved to a training base for the next four months. We packed everything up, loaded it onto a big truck, and set off. Our next stop wasn't far, but the landscape was completely different.

After a forty-five-minute drive, we arrived at our new home. We headed north from Hebron toward Jerusalem, then followed Route 1, a main highway running from Tel Aviv to Jerusalem, and then from Jerusalem to the Dead Sea. As we moved farther from Jerusalem to the east, the lush hills gave way to the arid desert, and eventually, we made a right turn onto a narrow dirt path. Another ten-minute drive took us to our destination: a base in the middle of the Judean Desert.

Upon arrival, we were told to wait on the bus until our commander confirmed the exact building that we would be in. I glanced outside and saw the desert stretching out around us, with gusts of wind blowing sand in every direction. It was the beginning of July, and summer was at its peak. Moments later, we stepped off the bus into the hot desert air. I felt like a loaf of dough being placed in a hot oven.

Welcome to Nebi Musa, our home for the next few months. The base is named after the prophet Moses. (*Nebi* means prophet and *Musa* is the Arabic form of Moses.) The only things around were camels, Bedouins, and, of course, soldiers like me. During the summer months, temperatures here regularly exceed 100°F, and I'm still trying to understand Celsius, but trust me, it gets really, really hot.

During this period, we were occasionally reassigned to guard duties, such as a week in Homesh in July and a month in Horesh Yaron near Ramallah in September. As a Lone Soldier, I also took a *meyuchedet*—a special leave—to visit my family in New York for a month in August 2023. This was my second time visiting home during my service. Upon returning to Israel in September, I only had a few months left in my service, as my release date was January 3, 2024. After my battalion finished our training period on Nebi Musa, we were scheduled to begin *kav* on the Gaza border starting November 5.

But fate had other plans. On October 7, 2023, the war began. My unit, instead of starting *kav* along the Gaza border in November, was inside the Gaza Strip itself. Reflecting back, I now realize how fortunate I was to have been in New York just weeks before the war erupted. Furthermore, I realize how fortunate I am that the war didn't begin a month later. If so, I would have been stationed along the Gaza border at its onset, and who knows what could have happened to me.

In the week leading up to October 7th, my battalion was preparing for a Targad (training exercise) stationed on the Nebi Musa training base. Everything was routine until that fateful morning when the world turned upside down.

CHAPTER 4

PREPARING FOR WAR WEEK

Jordan Valley, February 15, 2023

One step…another step…and yet another step. One foot after the other, as if my brain had stopped working, my body detached from my mind, and my legs were running on autopilot. I took another step, and then another, and then another.

At this point, water didn't interest me—I was beyond thirsty. My stomach had stopped growling because hunger was an afterthought. My dreams and aspirations were but dust, insignificant compared to the endless horizon of steps and unknown distances ahead. I was weighed down by nearly one hundred pounds on my back, yet I kept moving forward. Another step.

While real war is far more dangerous and comes with irreversible consequences, War Week in the IDF is more grueling physically, mentally, and emotionally. It breaks us down, pushes us to our absolute limits, and leaves little room for mercy or empathy from our commanders. During this week, the only real enemy is the unrelenting commands, and War Week itself becomes the ultimate test of endurance.

After countless steps, we had trekked nearly fifteen kilometers. Most of that distance wasn't just with the hundred pounds on our backs—it included the added challenge of a "stretcher walk." This is a classic IDF practice: a commander points to a soldier and shouts, "Drop injured!" For everyone else, this translates to, "You've got to be kidding me."

At this moment, the entire team halts, retrieves the seven-kilogram stretcher, and opens it. The "injured" soldier, along with their gear, is placed on the stretcher, and the team lifts it into the air. If we're lucky, it's just one soldier. Sometimes, multiple soldiers are declared "injured," and the burden multiplies. At any given time, four soldiers carry the stretcher while the rest rotate in and out, all while still hauling their own equipment. And, unfortunately, the commanders don't always choose the scrawniest, lightest team member to be "injured," if you know what I mean.

We never knew how much farther we had to go—that was part of the commanders' mind games. After walking fifteen kilometers, we reached the base of a massive hill—or, more accurately, a mountain. And if there's a mountain, we knew what that meant for us.

We are infantry soldiers more than anything else. We learn how to jump from a plane (it's our specialty). But walking is the main way we get from point A to point B. So, walking, we started climbing this monstrosity, a deceptively towering peak that only revealed its true scale as we ascended. Eventually, even the commanders realized how intense it was and told the "injured" soldier to get off the stretcher. Magically, that "injured" soldier wasn't "injured" after all. Who knew? Still, even without carrying the stretcher, the climb was relentless. Just when we thought we'd reached the top, another steep ascent would appear. And then another. Finally, as the sun set, we reached the peak.

It was a freezing winter night in the Jordan Valley. From the mountaintop, we could see the mountains of Jordan in the distance. The wind howled mercilessly, cutting through every layer of clothing. The long trek caused us all to sweat, and now that sweat had turned cold, pressing against our skin. I think I, more than anyone, felt it—ironic for a New Yorker, who should have been used to winter weather. The cold was so brutal that even though we were given a few hours to sleep, I couldn't. My limbs were numb, my body wouldn't stop shivering, and I couldn't calm myself enough to rest. While others lay on the ground, I paced back and forth, moving my limbs, trying desperately to regain feeling in my body.

That night, thankfully, was the final challenge of that War Week. The following day, back at base, I threw up several times and spent the entire weekend sick. I believed I might have had hypothermia. In retrospect, I certainly came down with hypothermia. If there's ever been a time in my life when I felt utterly broken—cold to my core—it was that week.

Welcome to a Targad, a battalion-wide War Week. Every eight months, the 890th Battalion of the Paratrooper Brigade is tested. On what, exactly? As the commander of the Paratrooper Brigade puts it, each battalion is evaluated on its readiness for war. How prepared are we to walk endless kilometers? To encounter terrorists? To sleep in unbearable conditions? To take over a neighborhood, search for threats, and protect one another? And, most importantly, how ready are we for Lebanon? Yes, Lebanon. The focus is always on our readiness for the Iran-backed Hezbollah militia in the north. Ironic, because during my service, these exercises prepared me for combat in Gaza, not the northern front.

This test is so significant that it's split into two weeks. The second week is War Week itself. It's the week where we walk endless kilometers, shiver to our core, and question our mere existence.

The week before, however, is entirely dedicated to its preparation. For an entire week, before the actual Targad, my battalion was stationed on base preparing for the hell week to come. It's a week to prepare both physically and mentally, understanding that the comforts we enjoy now are not going to be accessible to us in the following week. With every warm meal, shower, and mattress, we appreciate the small comforts.

We endure a Targad every eight months. Therefore, if you do the calculations, since the previous Targad was February 2023, the following was scheduled for eight months later…October. In fact, not only was our Targad scheduled for October, but specifically for October 7, 2023, the day the Jewish people will remember forever.

When Shabbat and the holiday of Simchat Torah ended that evening, we were supposed to hit the fields and begin our War Week test. The week before, from Sunday, October 1 until Friday, October 6, my battalion was stationed on base with the sole purpose of preparing for the Targad. Essentially, without even knowing it, we were preparing for the real war that was about to come.

Our weapons, obviously, are most important. If you enter enemy territory without a working gun, well, that's a problem. Early that week we all went to the shooting range and made sure not only that our weapons worked but also that they were calibrated with the scope, which means that the gun shoots where you aim. To do this we shoot at a target, aiming for a specific dot. Based on where our bullets land shows how we need to calibrate the scope. Once fixed, we shoot again. If the bullets hit the point at which we are aiming, our gun is calibrated and ready to go.

Once our guns are working, next comes the most "fun" part: cleaning our weapons. With cloth, oil, brushes, and a variety of other tools, we make sure that our weapons are spotless. Guns build up black residue when they're used, and if this residue builds up, the gun doesn't work as well. Furthermore, and especially in Israel, dust, sand, and dirt often accumulate inside the gun. Before heading into a war, and especially this War Week, ensuring our guns are clean is a top priority.

Each person on my team is given a specialty, and those specialties make up the team. Obviously, some are commanders and some are medics, but others are given special weapons. Some are sharpshooters, others have grenade launchers, and a few carry rockets, the Loa and Matador. The Loa is a smaller rocket weighing only a few kilos, and the Matador is huge, weighing 10.325 kilos, a fact I know simply because I carried this monstrosity many times during training. A few are given less appealing roles like the one carrying the stretcher, an annoying but necessary task. I, however, was given something a little cooler.

I was a Negevist. Weighing 7.6 kilograms, the Negev is an Israeli-made, lightweight machine gun. With its high-power automatic function and its lighter weight, carrying the Negev is one of the most sought-after roles on any team. One of the Negevists' main jobs is to protect the commander and essentially be their personal bodyguard. Throughout my time in Gaza, I'd find myself in the front alongside my commander. As he figured out our next moves, I stood beside him with my weapon up and my head swiveling in all directions.

Most soldiers in the Paratrooper Brigade use an M4 rifle. The M4 is based on the previous M16 rifle produced at the Colt's Manufacturing Company in Connecticut. These weapons have an automatic function, but within the IDF, we only use its semiautomatic capability. My friends who carried an M4 brought with them six magazines, each carrying thirty 5.56 caliber bullets, for a total of 180 bullets. I, on the other hand, had to carry four packs of 150 bullets each, and then another two chains each with eighty bullets. Into a war, I was required to carry at least 760 bullets. While the Negev was certainly sought after, it wasn't for the weak.

The week before the Targad required making sure that everything from the Negev was in its place. Not only did I need to shoot the gun and make sure it worked, but I also had to clean it well, and it's a much bigger and more complicated weapon than the M4. Additionally, I had to make sure I had all my bullets and that the chains were clean and aligned, so a jam wouldn't occur while I was shooting.

Beyond our weapons, we tested all of our gear and ensured every detail—down to the strings on our vests—met the battalion's high standards. I had to make sure my night vision worked, and that it linked to the scope on my weapon. I had to make sure my helmet fit well, my knee pads were on tight, and that my vest had every piece of equipment required. These tasks might seem small, but the point was to have every part of our equipment in order, and that sheer task could often cause a great deal of stress.

At the end of the week, all of this preparation culminates in *Misdar Magad*, where the battalion commander, or *magad*, personally inspects each soldier's equipment and gun. Going one by one, the *magad* clearly doesn't have time to check all of everyone's equipment. Not knowing what he'd check, we had to make sure everything was done well. If most of your equipment was good, but one thing wasn't, and he checked that one thing, depending on the severity, punishments can follow.

Mainly, though, especially for a Negevist like myself, the *magad* prioritized checking the cleanliness of the weapon. If he found black residue inside the gun, it meant I hadn't done my job well. Thankfully, I passed, but that moment was scary.

When Friday, October 6, 2023, arrived, there was excitement in the air. Shabbat and the holiday of Simchat Torah were upon us, offering a rare day of rest.

Holidays and Shabbat are always celebrated in the IDF, even if every soldier isn't religious himself. Operational responsibilities always come first, of course, but holidays and Shabbat are celebrated as much as possible, always. (In the IDF, there are both religious and secular Jews, and even a few non-Jews. And, in case you're wondering, most of the people on our base were men—and all combat soldiers on our base were men—but there were a few women in support roles.)

From Friday afternoon until Saturday evening, we had no schedule or obligations—a perfect opportunity to recharge before embarking on a War Week. But before releasing us, our commanders conducted one final check of our equipment to ensure we were ready. We had to leave our packed bags next to our beds, so that by the time Shabbat ended, all we needed to do was fill our camelbacks with water, strap on our gear, and start walking.

And so, we were ready—more ready than we'd ever been. Most Shabbats, our war bags aren't ready to go, our guns aren't spotless, and our minds aren't fixated on war. But this Shabbat was different. Even if our preparation was for a war simulation, we were mentally and physically ready for the real thing. As fate would have it, the following morning would test that readiness in ways we couldn't have imagined.

On the night of October 6, as Shabbat was beginning and the sun set, I made my way to Kabbalat Shabbat services (the prayer service that welcomes Shabbat each week). As I said, not only was it Shabbat, but it was also Simchat Torah, which meant a huge celebration. Hundreds of guys danced with Torahs, celebrating joyously. After Kabbalat Shabbat we moved into a larger room for the *hakafot*, the rounds of Torah dancing. At some point, dinner was served, and many of us headed to the dining hall, while others continued dancing. The next thing we knew, those dancing with the Torahs brought the party into the dining room, and the *hakafot* were happening right around us.

Why do I mention this? Because when tragedy strikes, you always remember where you were when it happened, and you always remember the calm before the storm. Many people can tell you exactly where they were when they heard about 9/11, or when they learned about Yitzhak Rabin's assassination. For me, October 6, the night before the storm, was that moment of calm.

Friday night was like any other, and there was a sense of normalcy in the air. Hundreds of guys dancing with Torahs might not seem calm, but there was something comforting about it. The next day, we were supposed to leave for a major exercise—a week meant to evaluate our battalion's readiness for war. But none of our speculations about the upcoming week were accurate.

That night, we hung out, talked, and speculated about what would happen and what challenges would be thrown our way. Some of my friends played soccer, others walked around the base. It was our first free night of the week, and we took advantage of it. We stayed up late, as our plan was to sleep in as late as possible on Saturday so we would be well-rested for the Targad starting Saturday night.

I went to sleep around 12:30 a.m., which wasn't too late, but others stayed up much later. We chatted, relaxed, and worried about the upcoming week. Little did we know, while we were speculating about our Targad, Hamas had their own plans. At 6:29 a.m. on October 7, 2023, we found out exactly what those plans were. The world would find out what their plans were.

Buzz, buzz, buzz...

It was Saturday morning, 6:29 a.m., and my phone vibrated relentlessly on the table beside me. I reached over, picked it up as it charged, and glanced at the screen. Alerts of incoming rockets into Israel flooded my notifications. I scrolled through them, scanning the locations, keeping an eye out for Kibbutz Erez, the community I had called home for the past couple of years.

I told myself, *Israel always deals with rockets. This is nothing new.* I silenced my phone, set it back down, and rolled over. I needed more sleep before that night's war week began. But as much as I tried, sleep refused to come.

Across the room, I heard my friends waking up as their phones buzzed to life, lighting up with the same alerts. I think we all understood that rockets are not a big deal, but the sheer level of red alerts was certainly abnormal. Around 6:45 a.m., the door to our room burst open. A commander entered.

"There's a situation in the south and we need to be ready," he said.

His words didn't fully sink in. For me—for all of us—it would take weeks, even months, to truly comprehend the magnitude of what was happening. But right then, all we knew was that something was unfolding in the Gaza region, and we had to prepare for anything and everything.

There was an understanding that everything was unknown, and at the very least our responsibility was just to be ready. In case we were needed, just be ready, be available. That's what we did.

Within moments, we were on our feet, rushing around to check our gear. My equipment was practically ready, as it was prepared for War Week, but then the commanders hit us with an unexpected instruction.

"Quickly pack a bag with personal items," they ordered. "We don't know when we'll be back. It could be next week before we return."

I didn't realize it then, but I would never set foot there again. The bag I threw together in a hurry would eventually find me at another base a week and a half later, while the rest of our belongings stayed at Nebi Musa. It wouldn't be until March—long after I had left Gaza—that I'd see these items again.

As we scrambled to gather our things, a friend said, "Look at this!"

I hurried over and watched a video on their phone. On the screen, we watched one of the first videos that circulated from that morning. Terrorists in Sderot, a small Israeli city along the Gaza border, stood on the back of a pickup truck, firing at buildings in the city. For the first time, it dawned on me—this wasn't just rockets. Something far worse was happening. However, my understanding of the situation was far from what it turned out to be.

Shortly after, our phones were collected (during certain operational responsibilities we weren't permitted to have our phones with us so we weren't distracted by them, and we wouldn't have them at all while we were in Gaza; our complete attention was on the mission). I wouldn't see mine again until October 15, more than a week later. From that moment on, anything I knew of the situation in Israel came from the ground. I was no longer following the war on my phone or the news—I was living it.

Our company commander called us into formation. We stood in the shape of the Hebrew letter *chet*—which is a squared off "n"—as he delivered a short briefing. The *chet* formation is when soldiers stand in a square with one side open, and the commander stands alone on that open side. The base of the *chet* has any number of soldiers, but the two sides must be equal in number. This is what usually happens, but as you can probably imagine on that morning, a sloppy *chet* was formed.

"We're taking all of our equipment and heading outside the base," he said. "Helicopters will bring us to the Gaza region. I don't know what the task is or where exactly we're going. But whatever mission we're given, we will carry it out to the best of our ability."

It was the kind of speech commanders gave when there were more questions than answers. By then, rumors were spreading about our destination. The early rumors indicated we'd be heading to Netiv Ha'asara, a *moshav*—a town—across the road from Kibbutz Erez.

Netiv Ha'asara is known for its Peace Wall, where visitors place mosaics with messages of hope and peace. From there, you can see into Gaza—a stark reminder of the area's tensions. I later learned that some of the first terrorists to enter Israel came through this community, crossing the border by paragliding.

Soon we walked outside our base, and by 9:00 a.m., we reached an open field where the helicopters were supposed to arrive. Despite our readiness, we ended up waiting for another ninety minutes. Only later, on a television program called *Uvda*, Israel's version of *60 Minutes*, in an episode about my unit and our October 7th story, I learned that the delay wasn't due to the helicopters—they were ready to go.

In normal situations, commands in the IDF flow from the top down. The headquarters, located at the Kiriya base in Tel Aviv, issues orders that are carried out across the chain of command. Apparently, the helicopters were prepped and ready for any mission but were waiting for specific instructions. Due to the *balagan* (craziness) that day, that command never came.

The *mahat*, or Paratrooper Brigade commander, contacted those in the Air Force directly to request helicopters. With an understanding that hundreds of soldiers were waiting for an airlift to the Gaza region, the pilots decided to act, and soon the helicopters were on their way.

We sat in the middle of the desert, speculating about what might be happening in the Gaza Envelope. Without our phones, we had no idea what was going on. Rumors spread that instead of heading to Netiv Ha'asara, we might be sent to Kibbutz Sa'ad, another community nearby that I knew well. Before enlisting I attended an *ulpan*, an intensive Hebrew course, in Sa'ad, just ten minutes away from Kibbutz Erez.

Nothing was certain. Sitting on the desert sand, we had more questions than answers. What we did know was that terrorists had entered Israel, though we didn't know how many or the scale of their attack. We assumed they had breached one or a few points and possibly reached some nearby communities. Based on that, we believed the IDF wanted troops to sweep each community thoroughly, search for any terrorists, and then secure the area until the threat was deemed to be over.

I'd been through similar situations before. A few months earlier, while serving in Hebron, there were repeated threats to communities like Kiryat Arba and Harsina. Once, there was suspicion of a terrorist in Harsina, and our entire base was called up. We split into teams, searched the area, and found nothing—it turned out to be a false alarm. We thought we were in for something similar that day: search a kibbutz, likely find nothing, and move on. We couldn't have imagined the scale of the attack—or the sheer number of terrorists we would encounter.

Later that morning, the sound of approaching helicopters broke the quiet. A murmur spread through our group. It wasn't excitement for what lay ahead—we still didn't fully grasp what was happening—but relief that we were finally moving.

Leading the way, our company boarded the first helicopter that arrived. It was a Yas'ur, an American-made helicopter introduced to Israel in 1969. These helicopters, used for transport, have been a part of Israel's history for decades. The Yas'ur isn't the largest helicopter, but it's not small either. Under normal circumstances, it fits about thirty soldiers, seated along two benches lining the sides. But that morning, with chaos all around us, the circumstances certainly weren't normal.

With over two hundred soldiers and only four helicopters, we crammed in as tightly as possible. Along with our bodies, we had massive bags and guns that needed space too. I was one of the first to board, finding a spot along the side. As more soldiers piled in, the helicopter ended up holding over fifty paratroopers—nearly double its standard capacity.

We were packed like sardines, with soldiers along the sides and the rest squeezed into the middle aisle, sitting practically on top of one another. Movement was impossible; I remember my leg being bent in an awkward position, unable to shift even slightly, and cramping.

The roar of the helicopter's engine meant communication was limited. Before takeoff, the crew gave us a quick briefing, but most of it was lost in the noise. We still didn't know exactly where we were headed. Rumors again swirled that our destination had changed, this time to Kibbutz Nahal Oz. Nahal Oz, located directly on the Gaza border near the Shejaiya camp, was a place I'd often seen in the news. Its residents lived just meters from constant danger, embodying resilience in the face of an unimaginable reality. Still, we didn't know if Nahal Oz was our actual destination or if this was just another rumor. The plan seemed simple: land, get our task, and execute it—nothing new, nothing extraordinary.

But as we took off, it became clear we weren't heading to Netiv Ha'asara, Sa'ad, or even Nahal Oz. Instead, fate—or Hamas—had other plans for us.

CHAPTER 5

HELICOPTER INCIDENT

Across from Kibbutz Alumim, October 7, 2023

Disoriented and trying to make sense of what had just happened, I heard the helicopter crew shouting, *"Koolam le'mata, koolam le'mata!"*—"Everyone down, everyone down!"

We scrambled to crouch down, keeping our heads below the line of windows. Before I could fully process what was happening, the sharp *ping* of bullets striking the helicopter's metal exterior rang in my ears. In that chaotic moment, it all became clear.

Our helicopter had been hit. The same helicopter that picked my unit up from Nebi Musa, the same helicopter that brought us to the Gaza Envelope to defend against Hamas's October 7th onslaught, had been hit by a hand-propelled rocket targeted directly at our helicopter. The helicopter shook, and we all fell to the ground. Now, as we crouched down below the line of windows, we were under attack again, but this time by gunfire.

My curiosity got the better of me. Turning my head slightly, I glanced around at my friends, all crouched down like me. I swiveled my head toward the closest window, but from my low angle, all I could see was the clear blue sky. I forced my eyes back to the ground and waited for further instructions.

At that moment, in the cockpit, the pilot made a heroic decision. He understood that bullets were flying in our direction, and with a massive fuel tank on board, we were in a dangerous situation. If, G-d forbid, a single bullet penetrated the tank while we were still airborne, the helicopter would explode in an instant.

Acting swiftly, the pilot activated a mechanism to detach the fuel tanks from the chopper, dropping them to the ground below. This potentially lifesaving move made one thing clear: An emergency landing was inevitable.

Compounding the danger, the pilot quickly realized that one of the engines had failed—most likely hit by enemy fire—leaving the helicopter operating on a single engine. With this added danger, the need for an emergency landing became even more urgent.

Bullets continued to strike the helicopter's exterior, and before we knew it, the same windows I had curiously gazed through just moments ago—those same windows that had framed my aerial tour of Israel—became entry points for Hamas bullets. The rounds shattered the glass and ricocheted around us. We stayed low, pressed against the floor. Moments later, with bullets still pinging off the chopper, we landed.

It wasn't a crash, but it was far from a soft landing. There was no doubt about the urgency of our situation. We faced a choice: remain in the helicopter, which offered some protection against the relentless gunfire, or evacuate into the open, where the battlefield awaited. With over fifty soldiers crammed into this tin-can target, the helicopter was as much a shield as it was a potential death trap. If another rocket struck, the consequences would be catastrophic. The decision was clear and immediate: We had to disembark and engage.

The crew worked to open the rear door to release us, but the mechanism failed. After several attempts and alternative methods, they finally managed to open the door manually—a last-resort measure that proved the damaged state of the aircraft.

As I crouched in the middle of the helicopter, I watched my friends ahead of me grab their bags and sprint outside. I inched forward carefully, staying below the line of windows as best I could. We knew there were terrorists in front of us, and there could be more to our left, though the soldiers farthest in that direction were covering from there. When my turn came, I hoisted my bag over my right shoulder and bolted. The bag, intentionally slung on my right side, served as makeshift protection—G-d forbid a bullet came my way, the bag stood as a shield.

Once I was far enough from the helicopter, I dropped to the ground, placing my bag between myself and the terrorists. The enemy was positioned in Kibbutz Alumim and along Route 232, roughly 100 to 150 meters away. The road was lined with trees, obscuring their exact location, but their presence was unmistakable as bullets rained down on us.

I positioned my machine gun, aiming toward the threat. At this point there was no order, no central command. Soldiers scattered in every direction, forming a chaotic pattern. Some of my friends were in front of me, others behind, to my left and to my right.

The Hamas bullets kept coming. I couldn't fire back yet; soldiers were in my line of sight, so it wasn't safe to shoot. My friends in the front, however, began returning heavy fire toward the terrorists.

As more soldiers exited the helicopter, bullets zipped over our heads, striking the ground around us. I glanced to my right, watching as the last of my comrades disembarked, one by one. The last soldier found himself tangled in a strap inside the chopper, struggling to break free. My commander, positioned right beside him, quickly stepped in to help untangle him. Once freed, they sprinted out together, the final soldiers to escape the damaged helicopter. Barely moments later, a whoosh pierced the air, followed by a massive, earth-shaking boom.

The helicopter had been hit again.

I turned my head to the right to look at the same vessel that had carried us from relative calm into a war zone. Flames engulfed the chopper, consuming it entirely. In an instant, it began burning down to its core. That decision, just moments earlier, to leave the helicopter rather than stay inside, had saved all our lives.

In front of me, the commander of our company lay beside one of the soldiers manning the MAG, a massive and powerful machine gun. The soldier was ordered to unleash its full force, firing relentless rounds in the direction of the terrorists. Behind them, the rest of us began to position ourselves in a row facing the terrorists, one by one, each several meters apart. We placed our bags in front of us, creating makeshift shields in the middle of this wide-open dirt field.

Though not as solid as rock or concrete, the bags proved to be life-saving barriers. Days later, some of my friends discovered both bullet holes and actual bullets lodged inside their bags—clear evidence that those shields had absorbed deadly shots during the firefight. Without them, the outcome could have been much worse.

Moments later, the commander and the MAG soldier sprinted back to join the rest of us. With everyone in position, we launched a unified return of fire, fighting back with all we had.

The tension was high, and my adrenaline surged. I'd been to shooting ranges countless times during my service, but this time was different. This time, I could hear bullets streaking over my head. It wasn't just practice—I felt like I was the target itself. Except this wasn't a feeling; it was reality. In the vast, open field, we could see puffs of dirt erupt every time a bullet struck the ground. The atmosphere was surreal, like a scene ripped straight from a war movie.

I was ordered to sprint to the far right and take a position at the edge of our row, closest to the helicopter but still at a safe distance. My role was clear: as the one carrying the Negev, I needed to cover a wider range. Positioned at the end of the line, I could fire both forward and to the right.

I dashed to my spot, dropped to the ground, and quickly positioned my weapon. Beside me, another soldier—a fellow American—was crouched, returning fire. I yelled over to him, "I feel like we're in a f***ing movie! What is this? Are those all terrorists?" Still processing the chaos around me, I could barely believe what I was seeing.

"Yes!" he shouted back between bursts of gunfire. With that, the gravity of our situation hit me. I gripped my Negev and started firing toward the enemy.

To my right, just tens of meters away, the sight of the helicopter we had just escaped caught my attention. Flames engulfed it completely, a fiery monument to the chaos we had barely survived.

For the next ten minutes, I lay flat on the ground, lined up with my comrades, with only our bags screening us from the gunfire. The burning helicopter raged to my right as I unleashed heavy fire in the direction of the enemy. I kept glancing to my left, waiting for new commands. Because we were exposed in the middle of this open field, I knew further instructions would come soon.

Behind us in the field, farther from the terrorists, the other helicopters from Nebi Musa landed. Unlike ours, these avoided being hit by Hamas rockets, allowing the soldiers to disembark safely. However, since they landed behind our position, these soldiers couldn't engage the terrorists directly because we were in front, and if they began shooting toward the enemy, they'd be shooting in our direction.

I continued shooting toward the terrorists, periodically glancing to my left, waiting for commands. To the left of our force lay a small, wooded area with scattered trees and rocks. Eventually, the decision came to make our way there. The rationale was clear: While we were currently in an open field, fully exposed to enemy fire, the forest offered some degree of cover and protection.

As the farthest on the right, I started the movement. I stood up, slung my bag over my shoulder, and sprinted left, plopping down again to fire toward the enemy. My friends to the right followed suit, running past me in staggered intervals. We repeated this leapfrog maneuver several times. Each time I stood, slung my bag, and advanced left, adrenaline was high.

Then, my commander gave me a direct order: Make a beeline for the trees. The distance was farther than my earlier sprints, but I didn't hesitate. With my bag over my right shoulder, I forced my legs into motion, my heart pounding as bullets zipped through the air. The ground seemed endless, and I felt exposed for an eternity. Every step carried the risk of one bullet or a stumble spelling disaster.

Looking back, I saw bullets kicking up dirt where I'd just been. I pushed on, summoning every ounce of energy I had left. Finally, I reached the edge of the forest, dropped my bag, and heard my commander again.

"Run forward! Get to the front line!" he yelled, pointing toward the trees nearest the enemy.

Grabbing my gun, I ran, darting past the chaos around me. As I advanced, I heard shouts: "*Josie nafal patzuah! Josie nafal patzuah!*"— "Joe is hurt! Joe is hurt!"

The words rang in my ears as I glanced back, searching for my friend Joe in the madness, but I couldn't locate him. Joe was the one friend who both served with me and was a part of my same *garin* on Kibbutz Erez. By this point, we'd already known each other for a few years. I pushed forward, focusing on the task at hand.

I finally reached my position, dropped to the ground behind a tree, and aimed my weapon toward the road where we knew the terrorists were hiding. Around me, our company executed a clear plan. With uncertainty about other enemy positions, we set up a 360-degree defense, with soldiers facing every possible direction. My assigned direction was toward the road, where we knew the enemy threat loomed largest.

It turned out that Joe had been shot. Since I had already moved forward, I couldn't locate him through all the craziness. The fear I had while lying in the open field and sprinting toward the forest became a reality for my friend. A bullet had struck him, but the medic on our team jumped in immediately and treated him right there in the field. From there, Joe was taken to one of the helicopters behind us, one that hadn't been hit and destroyed like ours. He was airlifted to a hospital and treated.

About twenty minutes later, when things calmed down a bit, I turned to our medic and asked how Joe was doing. He told me it wasn't a big deal and that Joe would be fine. It wasn't until later that I realized how much of a hero our medic was. Treating Joe under fire and making sure he got out safely was no small thing. The medic was being modest. Thankfully, Joe recovered and is now doing well, back to living his life.

As for the helicopter crew, they also managed to evacuate and make it to one of the other helicopters behind us, escaping the war zone just like Joe. Our pilot had been shot in the leg during the chaos, but even he ended up being okay. In the end, those were the only two injuries from the entire situation. A miracle, if you ask me.

I pushed forward, joining my friends behind trees and rocks. We positioned our guns toward the enemy—toward Route 232, where we knew the terrorists were. This new position was far safer than lying exposed in the open field. The trees and rocks offered significant protection, and for the first time since landing, I felt a small measure of security.

We cautiously advanced closer to the road, then made another move forward. At one point, a soldier spotted a terrorist up ahead and shouted, *"Mechabel, mechabel!"*—"Terrorist, terrorist!"

Instinctively, about ten of us turned our guns in unison and opened fire. The lone terrorist, who had been sprinting toward us with a weapon in hand, was neutralized almost instantly. One moment he was charging, the next he lay motionless on the dirt of the forest.

We continued advancing, moving closer and eventually passing the fallen terrorist and confirming he was no longer a threat. We realigned ourselves, facing forward toward the road. Behind us, other soldiers maintained a 360-degree perimeter, ensuring that all angles were secure.

At some point—though I can't recall exactly when—IDF forces arrived in vehicles, coming from the direction of Kibbutz Sa'ad and moving toward Alumim, where the terrorists were positioned. They took over the primary engagement with the enemy. We remained on the ground, covering our area and staying alert, knowing that a terrorist could appear from any direction.

After about fifteen or twenty tense minutes, it became increasingly clear that the immediate threat had been contained. We prepared ourselves for the next task ahead.

That catastrophic situation could have ended much, much differently. It turned out that when our helicopter was hit in the air, the rocket struck its bottom, damaging one of the engines. If that rocket had hit the center of the helicopter while we were all inside, the outcome would have been much worse. If the pilot hadn't detached the gas tank in time and a bullet had penetrated it, the helicopter could have exploded. Furthermore, if the second rocket had hit while we were still inside, or during the evacuation, things could have been disastrous. And, with the rounds of bullets that flew in our direction, the potential for disaster was huge. Given everything that happened, the fact that only two soldiers were injured is beyond any expectation.

The helicopter incident made the news, as you can imagine. Many articles were written; several news reports produced. The pilot was interviewed and shared his perspective. Finally, on October 19, twelve days after the war began, *Uvda* aired a twenty-five-minute mini-documentary that covered everything from the decisions made by our commanders that morning until the rocket strike on our helicopter. The documentary ended just as my own story reached its pivotal moment, before we moved on to our next task. However, what we didn't know then was that we'd already saved an entire community.

Halfway between Netivot and the Gaza border sits a religious community, Kfar Maimon. Established in 1959, with a population of roughly five hundred, it is part of the Sdot Negev Regional Council. Before the attacks of October 7th, I couldn't have told you this place existed—and even on that day, I didn't know about it. I ended up having a significant influence on its people, though I didn't know about it until a few weeks after it happened.

During a phone call with my parents, they asked me about Kfar Maimon, and if I had heard about its amazing story. I told them I didn't know what they were talking about, and they told me. Apparently, it was my unit, and my helicopter, that had saved this community. As incoming rockets and alerts of terrorist infiltrations swept the nation, the residents of Kfar Maimon were told to lock themselves in their safe rooms. This was nothing out of the ordinary and followed the same protocol as every other community in the Gaza Envelope. Several members of the community stood guard, and as they looked out a few hundred meters away, they spotted a slew of terrorists across a wide field near Kibbutz Alumim.

With the sound of gunfire and the fear that these terrorists could make their way toward their community—and knowing that Hamas had already reached towns much farther from the Gaza border—Kfar Maimon was in a state of panic. They began calling the IDF, the police, and any other security forces they could reach, but they were told no one could come help. Kfar Maimon, at that point, was entirely alone.

As religious Israelis, they began praying and hoping that G-d would be with them. According to them, in a matter of minutes the terrorists could have reached their community, and their level of readiness was at an all-time high.

Suddenly, they saw something incredible. They watched as helicopters appeared out of nowhere and landed between them and the terrorists. They saw one of the helicopters get hit by a rocket. They watched as soldiers exited the aircraft, dropped into position on the open field, and returned fire. They witnessed these soldiers eliminate every last terrorist who, only moments earlier, had posed a direct threat to them. They, in short, watched *my* story.

The people of Kfar Maimon were saved by luck—and by the help of G-d. Being a religious community, they described this moment as if we—myself and my fellow paratroopers—were angels who had fallen from the sky, landing right between them and danger, making sure that even if those terrorists had planned to reach Kfar Maimon, our presence alone had prevented it from happening.

It turned out that in the craziest moment of my life—escaping a destroyed helicopter with bullets flying all around me—there were people watching this action-packed film live. And it turned out that without even stepping foot in Kfar Maimon, and without even knowing it existed until weeks later, my unit had been the key reason these people were saved.

They gave us an open invitation to come for a barbecue, and I just might have to take them up on it someday.

My battalion has five companies. I was in Company Aleph, and we also had Companies Bet, Gimel, and Daled, named after the first four letters of the Hebrew alphabet. The fifth company was called Mesayat or Plugat Ha'esh, the special company. They handled specialized tasks, like snipers, a Jeep team, and more.

In the early hours of that day, the entire 890th battalion was gathered at the Nebi Musa base, getting ready to head south. The first challenge was logistics—how would we all get there? Plugat Ha'esh had their Jeeps, so they left first thing in the morning. My company and the others waited outside the base for helicopters to arrive. This meant that from the very start, our battalion was divided.

Plugat Ha'esh went to the Nahal Oz IDF outpost. This base quickly became overrun with terrorists and turned into one of the main battlegrounds of the October 7th attacks. The battle there lasted hours. It was from Nahal Oz that the female hostages Liri Albag, Na'ama Levy, Karina Ariev, Agam Berger, and Daniella Gilboa were taken into Gaza. Plugat Ha'esh, one of the first units on the scene, fought bravely that day.

Traveling to the Gaza region by helicopter, the four remaining companies—Aleph, Bet, Gimel, and Daled—landed in the same area, even though, as you already know, my helicopter didn't exactly "land." After the chaos and initial fighting, while gathered in the forest by Kibbutz Alumim, our commanders had to decide on our next move. Several senior officers, including the *samgad*, the assistant commander of our battalion, worked out our orders. By then, our battalion was split again.

With Plugat Ha'esh still at Nahal Oz, Companies Gimel and Daled headed to Kibbutz Alumim, across the road. Alumim, while not as devastated as some other communities, still suffered a brutal attack. Most of the destruction was in the industrial area, where many foreign workers from Thailand and Nepal were either killed or taken hostage into Gaza. Israeli civilians, soldiers, and security personnel also lost their lives. Gimel and Daled worked to secure the kibbutz and prevent further loss.

While we waited in the forest, I lay down with my weapon, resting on a rock, scanning the distance for any sign of danger. Behind me, my commanders discussed our next steps. Each of us reunited with our equipment, one soldier at a time, and prepared for what was coming. Despite the tension, there were brief moments of calm. I pulled a snack from my bag and exchanged small talk with friends nearby, trying to make sense of what we'd just been through.

But the reality around us was far from calm. Rockets continued to fly overhead, and in the distance, loudspeakers blared *"Tzevah adom, tzevah adom,"* warning residents of incoming rockets.

Then, our commander gave the order: "Get up in two lines. We're heading south to a kibbutz."

I thought we were in the clear. Earlier that morning, I'd seen that one video of terrorists attacking Sderot and assumed they'd come through tunnels and targeted places without fences. Surely, I thought, kibbutzim, with their borders and security systems, would be safe. As we know now, I couldn't have been more wrong.

I imagined we'd walk south, secure a kibbutz, and stand guard to ensure no terrorists could breach its perimeter. It felt simple in my mind—a dangerous trek, sure, but straightforward.

We strapped on our gear and lined up in two lines with large gaps between each soldier. This was the way we learned to advance during training weeks, and now it felt more real than ever. For three kilometers, we marched with weapons raised and heads swiveling to check for threats. Unlike training, where it's easy to let your guard down, no one wavered. We all understood the danger.

We walked parallel to Route 232, far enough from the road to avoid being completely exposed. The sounds of rockets overhead and sirens in the distance rang in our ears, and the tension in the air was palpable. After about forty-five minutes, we reached a point where we were instructed to cross the road. As we stepped across, I realized exactly where we were.

We entered the Be'eri Forest. I'd been here before, back in February 2023, during the Darom Adom festival. The "Red South" was in full bloom then, and the ground was covered in a breathtaking carpet of red anemones, or in Hebrew, *kalaniyot*. Families and tourists had filled the trails, enjoying the beauty of the landscape.

Once we crossed, we stopped to switch from *kaved* (heavy) to *kal* (light). This meant dropping our large bags and keeping only the essentials in our vests: weapons, ammunition, water, first-aid gear, and a few other items.

It was around 1:00 p.m. None of us knew what was waiting for us inside Kibbutz Be'eri. A few small police units and elite IDF teams, like Shaldag, had made it in earlier, but they were vastly outnumbered. The kibbutz's own security team had been holding the line since the attack began.

While we didn't know it at the time, our two companies—over one hundred soldiers in total—were about to become the first major IDF force to enter Kibbutz Be'eri. As I stood outside its gates, waiting for the order to move, I had no idea what was on the other side—moments that would change my life forever.

CHAPTER 6

BE'ERI

Kibbutz Be'eri, October 7, 2023

"G uys, we need to be careful," my commander said. "This isn't Gaza or Lebanon. We aren't entering territory where it's just us and terrorists." He was right. We had just crossed into a place far more complicated than anything we'd dealt with before. Inside the gates of Kibbutz Be'eri were IDF soldiers, yes—but also the very Hamas terrorists responsible for the massacre. Beyond that, there were police officers, members of various Israeli security forces, the kibbutz's own security team, and most importantly, at 1:00 p.m. that day, the community was still full of Israeli civilians.

We need to be careful—it wasn't just a reminder. It was a warning.

The scale of what was happening inside Be'eri was still unknown to us. We had no phones, no news updates, and no real briefings from our commanders. No one could give us even a hint of what we were walking into. Just outside the kibbutz gate stood a mess of soldiers from all over the IDF. I didn't stop to see which units they were from, and I didn't have time to ask why they were just standing there and not going in.

Questions like those would have to wait.

By our side that day was a team from the esteemed Sayeret Matkal unit. Sayeret Matkal—or just Matkal, as most Israelis call it—is one of the most elite units in the IDF. They're the ones sent on the most secretive, sensitive, and dangerous missions. Their training is extensive—far longer and more demanding than anything I went through. While soldiers like me spent nights doing four-hour guard shifts in Hebron, Matkal soldiers were the kind you'd expect to be deep behind enemy lines.

But on that day, in this surreal and chaotic situation, they were right there, with us.

Despite the differences in training, experience, and status, none of that mattered now. We were all there for the same reason: to save Be'eri. Just moments before we crossed the gates ourselves, we watched as this team from Sayeret Matkal moved in ahead of us.

As we walked toward Be'eri, I still held onto the hope—maybe better described as the illusion—that once we reached the kibbutz, we'd be entering a kind of safety zone. It was fenced in, after all. I thought that meant security, protection. I imagined we'd arrive, locate the civilians, and defend them from the outside threat. Again, that assumption couldn't have been more wrong.

As we neared the gates of Be'eri, the sense of safety started to slip away. The sounds coming from inside—loud, sharp bursts of gunfire—spoke volumes. Still, nothing prepared me for the moment we stepped inside.

We entered in two lines, weapons up, eyes wide open. Just a few steps past the gate, I looked to my left and saw bodies on the ground. I didn't get close enough to see if they were Israeli civilians or Hamas terrorists, and at the moment, it didn't matter. What mattered was that they were dead—and that Be'eri, in that single moment, revealed itself not as a safe zone but as a full-blown war zone.

We moved quickly, making a right and hugging the perimeter of the kibbutz. Be'eri sits at the northern end of the Eshkol Regional Council. Established on October 6, 1946, it's one of the wealthiest kibbutzim in the region. Be'eri Print is the beating heart of its economy—printing everything from photo albums to credit cards, even Israeli driver's licenses. Every winter, thousands of Israelis travel south to see the red *kalaniyot* blooming in the Be'eri forest, turning the region into a sea of color. The Darom Adom festival, one of the biggest in the south, takes place just outside its gates.

But there were no flowers now. No tourists. No peace.

As we passed the gas station on our left, we reached a junction. Straight ahead was the outer fence. To the left, the center of Be'eri.

We turned left.

The sounds of gunfire intensified. The volume spiked, and it felt like the chaos was coming from all directions. Every corner, every alley, every house could be hiding terrorists. With each step deeper into the kibbutz, we understood we weren't arriving at the scene after the fact. We were walking straight into it.

We moved in two lines down a main road, weapons up, eyes scanning every angle—forward, left, right. The air was thick with tension, but we kept moving until we reached a courtyard. Houses encircled a patch of grass in the center, anchored by a large tree with branches stretched out wide, casting shade over the open space. On any other Shabbat—especially a warm, sunny day like that one—I could picture children playing on that lawn, their parents nearby, standing in kitchen windows sipping coffee, calling out gently to their kids to come inside for lunch.

But this Saturday was nothing like that.

What we saw instead shook me.

One of the homes surrounding the courtyard was completely

engulfed in flames. The fire raged so intensely that it was impossible to miss. But then, out of the smoke, we saw something we weren't prepared for—movement inside the house. A family. Through the window, they spotted us and began signaling for help. That moment marked our first direct encounter with the civilians of Be'eri, and we snapped into action.

One of Hamas's tactics was horrifying in its simplicity. Knowing that Israeli families would be hiding in their *mamadim*—safe rooms fortified with thick concrete and steel—Hamas would set the house on fire. The idea was to create a pressure trap. Inside, smoke would begin to build. Oxygen would disappear. The family would have to make a decision: stay inside and suffocate…or run outside, right into the terrorists' hands. If they chose the latter, Hamas would be waiting to kidnap or kill them.

We had no way of knowing if any terrorists were still lurking nearby, but there wasn't time to hesitate. A decision had to be made. With weapons raised and other soldiers positioned to guard our surroundings, a few of us approached the house.

The family didn't need help escaping. They needed protection. Imagine that—your house is burning to the ground, and yet the bigger fear is what's waiting for you outside. That level of fear is something I don't think most people can comprehend.

We quickly escorted the family several doors down to a neighbor's house. Luckily, the distance between the homes was just enough that the fire wouldn't leap from one to the next. Once they were safe, we regrouped.

With our first mission in Be'eri a success, we pushed on, heading deeper into the heart of the kibbutz. The sounds of gunfire echoed somewhere ahead of us. Normally, when someone hears gunshots, instinct tells them to run the other way. But as combat soldiers, it pointed us toward where we were needed most.

We moved in two staggered lines, weapons raised, scanning in every direction. Suddenly, a voice called out from above. We looked up and saw two members of Be'eri's *kitah konenut*, the community's local security team, perched on a rooftop.

"Be careful!" one shouted. "They're everywhere—even on the roofs!"

It wasn't a command—it was a warning. A warning from someone who had seen this massacre unfold. The terrorists weren't just hiding inside homes—they were scattered everywhere. Behind fences, between trees, even above us. Every step we took could lead us straight into a terrorist encounter.

As we moved forward, we stopped frequently, whenever our commanders needed to reassess the situation. With each stoppage, our job was simple: secure the area. That meant dropping to our stomachs and pointing our weapons outward, creating a full 360-degree perimeter. Everyone had a sector to cover. Because I carried the Negev gun, I was always positioned in the front, aiming straight down the path we hadn't yet cleared. It was the riskiest direction. The most unknown. And that made my responsibility heavier than most.

In these high-stress, high-stakes moments, the human body doesn't just turn off. In other words, your basic needs don't wait for a more convenient time to show up. I've always been known for having a small bladder and I'd needed to pee since we first stepped foot inside the kibbutz. It sounds ridiculous, even a little shameful, if I say it out loud. There I was, in the middle of a battlefield, adrenaline pumping, bullets flying nearby—and all I could think about was how badly I had to go.

Finally, during one of our stops, I couldn't hold it in anymore. I turned to the soldier next to me and told him to take over my field of fire. "Cover me," I said, half-joking, half-serious. I shuffled a few steps to the side, turned toward a bush, and relieved myself while my friend watched my sector, weapon ready.

It was the most absurd moment in the most serious situation. But that's how war works. Life doesn't pause just because the world around you is falling apart. I remember that moment so clearly, not just because of the physical relief, but because it was one of those strangely grounding, humanizing flashes that reminded me I was still just a twentysomething-year-old guy—tired, nervous, and in need of a bathroom.

Months later, when I returned to Be'eri to visit, I walked past that same spot. I stopped, looked around, and pointed it out. "That's where it happened," I told the guy walking beside me. "That's the bush." Don't worry—I didn't go again. But I smiled. Somehow, in a place so heavy with loss and trauma, that memory stayed with me.

Up until that point, even though the sounds of war had surrounded us all day, I hadn't yet come face-to-face with Hamas. That was about to change.

Every kibbutz in Israel, beyond its quiet and communal way of life, is defined by its focus on family and youth. The children are the heartbeat of the place—the future of the community. From an early age, kids grow up together like siblings. They spend their days in the kindergarten, the after-school programs, or at summer activities, all centralized in a little section of the kibbutz dedicated entirely to them. On a normal weekday, that part of the kibbutz is bustling—parents dropping off and picking up their children and kids laughing and playing. But on Shabbat, the Jewish day of rest, the area goes still. The buildings are empty.

That's why, on that Saturday, the day of the attack, those buildings stood quiet. No children. No families. Just walls and silence. But that silence had been invaded.

Terrorists had taken over several of the kindergartens and fortified themselves inside. As we approached that section of the kibbutz, my team found cover behind a low concrete wall running along one of the main roads. To our left stood the dental clinic. Behind us, more kindergartens. And across the street, several more buildings meant for children, along with playgrounds.

The wall came up to about waist height, with garbage cans lined up on the far side. We crouched down behind it, my heart pounding in my chest. I dropped to my knees and set my Negev on top of the wall. Only my neck and head peeked out above. I scanned the scene through my scope, eyes locked on the buildings across the road.

Then—movement.

A man darted out of one of the buildings, grabbed a duffel bag from the ground, and ran back inside. He wore civilian clothes. I saw no weapon on him. My scope followed him the whole way, and my finger hovered over the trigger.

But I didn't shoot.

In that split second, the warning from my commander echoed in my head: "We need to be careful. This isn't Gaza or Lebanon."

This was Be'eri. Civilians were still here. The lines between enemy and innocent were dangerously blurred. I wasn't just afraid of being shot—I was terrified of shooting the wrong person. A mistake like that would live with me forever. If I died, it would be tragic. But if I pulled the trigger and took the life of someone I was meant to protect? That's a burden I couldn't carry.

So, I let him go. I simply didn't know.

And then, moments later, the same man—and whoever was inside that kindergarten with him—opened fire on us.

Bullets whizzed over our heads, slamming into the concrete wall and garbage cans. We ducked behind the wall, instinct taking over. My heart pounded harder now—not just from adrenaline, but from the gut-punch of confirmation. These weren't civilians. They were terrorists.

We raised our heads, took aim, and returned fire. It was less about eliminating a target and more about letting them know we were here— that we weren't going anywhere. Most of our bullets struck the exterior walls of the kindergarten. Maybe a few hit windows. But the building was fortified. We knew they were most probably still alive.

Only later did I come to understand what that duffle bag had likely contained: ammo. One of Hamas's tactics was to carry in as much fire-power as possible, stuffing extra ammunition, grenades, and equipment in duffel bags. Their plan relied on staying in the fight as long as they could, moving from home to home, building to building, with more than enough supplies to sustain them.

And another one of their signature tactics—the one that made fighting them so agonizing—was blending in. They wore civilian clothes to make it harder for us to tell who was who. This was a tactic Hamas used in Israel during the attacks of October 7th to blend in with our civilians in Israel, and in Gaza to blend in with their own. It doesn't matter where they are, Hamas hopes the IDF mistakes them as innocent.

Some even wore shirts with Hebrew writing on them. Those weren't difficult to get—thousands of Gazans had worked in Israel before the war. Almost none of them wore uniforms. A few had green Hamas bandannas, but that was it.

Looking back, I stand by my decision not to shoot that man. In the moment, I did what I thought was right. I could live with missing a shot at a terrorist. Either I'd get him later, or someone else would. But shooting an innocent Israeli? I couldn't come back from that. So I hesitated—and I'll never apologize for it.

In that war zone, with a loaded machine gun in my hands and chaos swirling around me, that choice defined something important. Not just what kind of soldier I was—but what kind of person I hoped to stay.

Kneeling behind that concrete half-wall, I kept my eyes fixed on the area in front of me. To our left stood the dental clinic. We could hear sounds coming from that direction, but it was impossible to see what was happening. A dense cluster of trees and bushes blocked our view. We didn't know it at the time, but a heavy battle was unfolding there as well.

Then, suddenly, things escalated.

Our company commander, sensing something suspicious across the road, made a decision. He selected a small squad of four and led them forward to strike. The rest of us remained behind, providing cover. My job was to keep my weapon pointed toward the road and watch for anything that might threaten them.

As they crossed, I tracked them through my scope. They made their way up a fence, just beyond which was a children's playground—bright colors, metal bars, little plastic slides, now ghostly in their silence. And then, movement.

A figure, lying flat behind several large crates filled with toys, suddenly lifted his arm. In one quick motion, he threw a grenade over the fence, in the direction of my friends. Time froze for a second.

They saw it, too—and immediately scrambled back, retreating behind whatever cover they could find. Without hesitation, I opened fire, joined by the soldier next to me. We unloaded round after round into the area where the grenade had come from. The terrorist was prone behind the crates, and with all the obstacles in the way, we couldn't see if he had been hit. But between the bullet holes in the fence and the volume of fire we laid down, we felt confident that he was either dead or at the very least seriously injured. In our eyes, that counted as a success.

We stayed positioned behind that wall for nearly an hour and a half, locked in place, constantly scanning. Every few minutes, we shot toward anything suspicious. Terrorists were clearly holed up in the buildings across the road, and we needed them to know they weren't in control anymore.

Eventually, we received the order to move. We shifted to a house across from a different playground, taking up a new position. Some of my teammates went upstairs to guard the park. They did what I had just been doing—scanning, watching, engaging. Several of them spotted terrorists and returned fire when needed, keeping them away from the nearby homes. I stayed downstairs near the front entrance, watching our backs, making sure no one entered inside unnoticed. It was a small job, maybe, but still important. In this kind of environment, even the smallest role could save lives.

Up until that moment, the fighting we had engaged in was unlike anything I'd experienced before—or would experience again. It was raw. Stripped of all the advanced systems and overwhelming power that usually defines the IDF.

Weeks later, when we entered Gaza, we finally saw what the full might of the IDF really looked like. It wasn't just us, the infantry men, with our guns slung across our shoulders. It was the Navy operating offshore, the Air Force providing air strikes overhead, tanks rolling through neighborhoods, artillery lighting up the sky, combat engineering units clearing paths and detonating threats—even dogs working alongside soldiers. Every branch moved together, forming a coordinated machine. It was efficient. It was effective. And, most importantly, it was safer for us on the ground.

But Be'eri, at that moment, wasn't like that.

In Be'eri, it was just us—boots on the ground, rifles in hand. Infantry soldiers against terrorists. Our guns versus theirs. No backup, no support, no overwhelming firepower from above. Just small teams of young men going house to house, facing terrorists doing the same.

Looking back, it was almost primitive in its simplicity—and terrifying because of it. There was no air strike coming to wipe out the threat ahead. Our skill was on display, not our firepower.

I'd never want to experience that kind of fighting again. The IDF's advantage over Hamas has always been its strength and firepower. But in Be'eri, stripped of all that, it came down to skill—ours versus theirs.

As the day wore on, the mood began to shift. When we arrived at Be'eri at around 1:00 p.m., we were the first major IDF unit to enter. By late afternoon, reinforcements began to arrive. Not just more regular soldiers but special forces and, finally, tanks.

With their arrival came a change in the air. For the first time all day, we weren't just reacting—we were taking control. The chaos remained, but there was structure now. There was momentum. The terrorists had to know it too.

As evening fell, my unit was given a new mission. One more important than any we'd had so far.

To rescue families.

While special forces and tanks targeted known pockets of Hamas presence, our job was to move from house to house, locate civilians still hiding in their safe rooms, and bring them out safely. The work continued through the night, long after the sun had gone down. It was slower, more deliberate, but in many ways more emotionally intense than anything we'd done earlier. These weren't theoretical people anymore. These were Israelis—parents, children, grandparents—trapped in homes where they had once felt safe.

This task became the most meaningful of all. In the face of destruction, fear, and death, it gave us something else to fight for. It reminded us why we were there.

✡ ✡ ✡

That day was a hot one. While Hamas's presence was felt throughout the Gaza Envelope, and terrorists were going door to door, one of the things overlooked quite often are the human needs. When it's time to eat or drink, use the restroom, or even take a breather from the intensity of combat. Human needs are integral to the success of any combat soldier.

We always carry a camelback in our vests, holding roughly three liters of water. Obviously, the length of time this water lasts depends on factors such as the weather and what one is doing. On October 7, 2023, we certainly weren't lying on the couch watching Netflix. The day was intense, and this required staying hydrated.

After situating ourselves in a house across from a playground, my team commander decided we needed to find water. The plumbing throughout the region was off, so there was no faucet to fill up our camelbacks. My commander took me and three other soldiers outside for a simple mission: find water.

With terrorists still everywhere in the kibbutz, we headed in the opposite direction of the gunfire. We arrived at a house and tried entering, but the door wouldn't budge. Next door was another house, and this door, too, wouldn't budge. My friend, standing next to me, gave several hard kicks to the door with his foot, and eventually, the door swung open.

We went inside searching for water, not expecting any civilians to be there. Hearing some noise from the shelter, we said, "*Tzahal, tzahal*"—"IDF, IDF"—and suddenly a young couple opened the shelter door and walked out. "We are here to rescue you," we told them. "You'll be coming with us."

Appearing by our side were two individuals, a man and a woman. They were of an age where they could be recently married, engaged, or just long-time boyfriend and girlfriend living together. The house was modest. There were no kids or anybody else.

We asked if they had any bottled water, and they gave it to us with smiles on their faces. Pulling out two six-packs from under the table, we now had six bottles of water and another six bottles of Coca-Cola, each bottle one and a half liters. With two civilians rescued and fluids to hydrate ourselves, we returned to the house with our entire team and considered this small mission a success.

For hours into the night, our goal remained to rescue civilians from their homes. We took the couple back to our home base, this one house in Be'eri. The task was to rescue families from neighboring homes, bring them back to our "home," place them in the safe room of the house, and, when there were enough civilians, take them either by vehicle or on foot outside the kibbutz to safety.

Before that, we had this young couple with us. The woman quickly went into the shelter. With a look of shock drawn across her face, it was clear she didn't want to engage in conversation. However, the man left the shelter for a few moments and came to us, the soldiers who had just rescued him. He started engaging in small talk, and then suddenly, realizing he had a phone on him, one of my friends asked for a news update.

Mind you, at this point, about 7:00 p.m., we hadn't seen our phones since the early morning. The only thing we knew, naturally, was what we saw in front of us with our own two eyes. He opened his phone and started going over the news: the death toll, the injured, the hostages, and the locations where Hamas had hit the hardest: Kfar Aza, Nir Oz, and right there in Be'eri.

As he finished, I turned to him quietly and asked for an update on Kibbutz Erez. All day I had been thinking of my own community. If what was happening in Erez was anything close to what was happening in Be'eri, surely, I had something to worry about. Friends of mine were there that weekend, and obviously my host family, whom I loved dearly. The man looked up Erez in the Google search bar and said, "I can't find anything on Erez, and for now that's a good thing." I obviously knew that not all could be good at Erez, and later I found out that Amir Naim lost his life that day. However, at that moment, hearing that Erez wasn't in the news gave me a huge sigh of relief.

As the night went on, the rescuing of civilians continued. Our team split into two. Half stayed in our current house and the other half went door to door. Once we had each family, they would be brought back to our house, protected, and from there taken outside the community's gates. The process of getting to them, however, wasn't so easy.

In the early moments of the war, all civilians within the Gaza Envelope were told to take shelter not only from incoming rockets but from an infiltration of terrorists. This doesn't only mean going into the safe room of the house, fortified with concrete to protect against rockets, but closing and locking the doors, shutting the windows, turning off the lights, lowering the blinds, and making sure that nobody, and I mean nobody, is able to enter.

So, you might be wondering how exactly we would rescue families. It wasn't as if we could knock on the front door and await a response. These civilians were not coming to the door. Just like we did earlier with the first family, we had to find a way to enter the house. This was either by getting through the front door, which many times was only possible by pushing or kicking it open, or even by climbing through the window, which I did twice. After getting inside, the next step was to approach the door of the safe room. Once there, things got interesting.

The last thing we wanted to do was open the door to the safe room where the family was hiding, and there are several reasons why. First of all, civilians were scared—scared that their lives might be taken and scared of who was on the other side of that door. Friends of theirs in neighboring houses faced similar situations, and their stories ended drastically differently. Instead of soldiers on the other side of the safe room door, it was terrorists. Instead of being taken to safety, their lives were taken at that moment, or they were taken hostage into Gaza. The last thing we wanted to do was startle them.

Second, we waited for the family to open the door themselves to protect ourselves. Many families brought some last-resort piece of defense into their safe rooms in case a terrorist came. Some families held knives; some even had a pistol. The last thing we wanted to do was put our own lives at risk. Therefore, the decision to open the door was left entirely up to the family.

After approaching the door of the safe room, we had to convince the family, through the door, that we were the good guys, that we were there to rescue them. Oftentimes the family, believing us, opened the door right away. That made it easy on us since we were able to quickly bring the family to safety. Sometimes, the convincing was a little harder.

Israeli civilians couldn't be sure who stood on the other side of the door, and they didn't want their decision to open the door to be the wrong one. If, G-d forbid, we were terrorists, they would have made a decision that ended their lives. There were Hamas terrorists who spoke Hebrew, so language wasn't always what convinced them.

At one home, my company commander stood by the safe room door and tried telling the family inside that he was a commander in the Paratrooper Brigade, and he was there to rescue them. Hearing no response, he told them his name and military ID number, to no response. He shared more details about himself, and still no response. Then, he decided to say, through the door of the safe room, the Shema Yisrael, a well-known prayer in Judaism. Only then, after several moments, did the family decide to open the door, finally believing him. This story shows exactly the mindset of families in Be'eri and throughout Israel that day. In other houses nearby, there were bodies lying on the floor, and the same situation had occurred in those houses as this one. The only difference was that instead of IDF soldiers standing on the other side, there were terrorists. Instead of being rescued, the civilians took their final breaths.

My entire service—from training, to standing guard in Hebron, to being yelled at by commanders for the dumbest reasons—was all worth it. If for nothing else but these moments. Knowing that these civilians were scared and worried for their lives. To know that until they saw soldiers in IDF uniforms, they didn't know if they would make it. And knowing that it was me and my team who played a huge role in keeping these civilians alive was all I could have asked for. I honestly felt like my service in its entirety culminated in those moments.

Throughout the night, we continued rescuing families. I spent most of the time in our home base, and civilians were brought to us, and we protected them while they waited in the safe room. At one point a family with two little kids entered, and with the sounds of gunfire all around, I saw the look of fear on their faces. Crouching down to their level, a skill I learned during my days working at camp, I assured these two children that all would be well, that they were now in the hands of soldiers. We were there to protect them, and while there was a lot to be scared about, this would pass.

As the night went on, despite the complexity of the situation at hand, I found a moment or two to doze off while others were keeping watch. I was able to sleep at one time for about half an hour. While not a lot, it was the only sleep I would get until much later in the night.

Just before midnight, my entire team regrouped with a band of civilians. The next step was to bring them outside of the kibbutz safely; this was, so we thought, the last group. In two spaced-out lines, our team prepared for movement. Since I had the Negev gun, I was placed in the front, next to our main sharpshooter. Advancing toward the gate, we walked past what earlier was the scene of a massacre and still was reminiscent of one. Passing dead bodies all around, the feeling was one straight out of a horror film. Looking forward, I had a huge responsibility on my shoulders: to help protect my fellow teammates as well as the families. At one moment, as we walked past burned cars, broken-down homes, and dead bodies, I took a peek behind me to glimpse at the civilians we were taking to safety. I watched as mothers and fathers placed hands over their children's eyes. With the sound of gunshots in the background, it was as if these parents knew they couldn't protect their children from the sounds of this massacre, but at the very least they could protect them from the sights of one. I turned my head to face forward and kept on moving.

Eventually we made it to the front gate of Be'eri. It was just after midnight, and we had now entered October 8. The last time I had seen the outside of this kibbutz was eleven hours earlier, and the change in the scene was literally night and day. At 1:00 p.m. on October 7, the scene outside of Be'eri was a scattered array of soldiers and police officers trying to figure out what was happening and what our next moves would be. Now, the outside of Be'eri had turned into what looked like IDF headquarters.

With tents set up with television screens, I watched as high-ranking IDF officials monitored the situation inside the kibbutz. Hundreds of people were in the area, all looking busy, all understanding that what was happening here was unique. The civilians were taken directly to a bus, and from there brought far away from the region. Eventually the residents of Be'eri were displaced to the area of the Dead Sea, but right then I wasn't sure where they went. We had just brought them outside of Be'eri, and our mission was complete.

Not long after that, our commander quickly gathered us together again. He told us that there were still several houses with known living civilians, so we had to go back. Without much hesitation, we regrouped, got in two lines, and reentered the kibbutz. Walking past the same burned cars, crumbled homes, and dead bodies, we made it back to the area of Be'eri where we had been earlier. We rescued two more families, one of whom required entering through a side window, and from there brought them outside the kibbutz. This took time, and we didn't cross the gates again until nearly 2:00 a.m.

For the first time since we arrived in the region by helicopter earlier that day, we finally felt we were in the clear. With IDF soldiers all around us, it was finally our chance to rest, at least a bit. Just past the kibbutz gate was a grassy area on the right, and my entire company made it there to lie down. Some of us tried closing our eyes, others just sat there and tried to relax. For the next half hour, I sat looking up at the sky, seeing the stars far away, and hearing gunshots in the distance.

Just before 2:30 a.m., our company commander stood us all up and asked us to gather around in the classic chet formation. "Listen," he told us. The sounds of battle still rang from inside the kibbutz. "While this has been the craziest day of our lives, and we are all tired beyond belief, our work is not over. You can still hear the gunshots from inside the kibbutz. We're going back in."

At this moment fear ran through me. I thought I had survived. It was clear, just by looking at the dead bodies throughout Be'eri, that not everyone had been so lucky. I thought that this was it, that this horror of a day had come to an end. All the adrenaline that had kept me going had disappeared. I was tired, it was dark, and I was beyond scared. The last thing I wanted to do was to once again walk in the direction of the fire, but I had no choice. While there weren't any more families to rescue, there were terrorists to eliminate.

In two lines, we entered Be'eri and made a right turn, just as we had more than twelve hours before. Walking past the gas station on our left, we continued along the kibbutz perimeter. Now, instead of turning toward its center as we had earlier that day, we continued farther along the edge. Finally, we were told to stop and given our next task.

While we thought we'd be engaging with the terrorists, our task ended up being a lot simpler. Dispersing ourselves along the fence of Be'eri closest to Gaza, we were to lie down, look forward, and protect the kibbutz border; essentially, to make sure no terrorists came close. Our company dispersed along the fence, each person lying down about five or ten meters from the next.

I mentioned earlier that it wasn't just IDF soldiers inside Be'eri that day, but rather anybody from the security establishment in Israel, such as police officers. The police also have special units, and several of them were on the front lines on Israel's darkest day. That morning, two vehicles from the Matpa unit of the Israeli police were operating in Be'eri. Nine soldiers split between two Jeeps. In the end, we learned eight of them lost their lives, and only one lucky man, the driver of one of the Jeeps, miraculously survived.

Outside, it was dark. I looked through my night-vision scope and scanned the area in front of me for any sign of movement. There weren't supposed to be any Israeli civilians or security forces in the open field between us and the Gaza border, and any movement most likely was a terrorist. Nonetheless, this was all in the dark of night, and this made the situation more complicated.

Right behind me sat one of the Jeeps, burned and destroyed to its core. It looked exactly the way our helicopter had hours earlier, but this was worse. Inside the Jeep sat the burned remains of police officers who woke up that morning hoping to return to their same bed at night. Police officers who went to protect their people and now were burned inside the confines of this vehicle. Right next to the Jeep lay a giant man on his stomach with his head facing into the ground. This man was built with muscles and clearly had the heart of a warrior. He lay there with no breath in him, and what appeared to be no significant burns. Probably, if I had to guess, this hero escaped the burning Jeep, unlike his friends, but was met with gunfire immediately after his escape.

The Jeep had been hit by an RPG; that's what caused the damage. Now, while my responsibility was to look forward and protect Be'eri from any additional threats, my mind was focused on what lay directly behind me.

We were positioned there along the kibbutz's perimeter for about an hour. The heat of the day turned into a cold night. At a certain point, a commander shouted for me to come. I ran over, a little shocked that he had asked for me, specifically, and he said a soldier from Shayetet, the Israeli version of the Navy Seals, needed "your help." *My help?* I wondered. *Why me?* Different units were given different tasks that night, and the most prestigious special forces were engaging with terrorists throughout Be'eri, while we, for example, at this moment guarded the border fence.

This Shayetet soldier, holding the same gun as me, a Negev, said he was running low on ammo. He asked for some, and I gave it to him. He was, after all, engaging with terrorists throughout the night, and don't worry, I made sure to keep more than enough for myself. This situation, more than anything else, perfectly illustrates how we were all working together that day. It didn't matter where in the IDF we came from; a threat was looming, and only by working together and helping one another could we get through it.

After about an hour we stood up from our position along the fence and moved behind a house on this exterior road. The house was burned to its core. Everything was black, the smell of ashes still fresh and poignant. The time was around 4:30 a.m. on Sunday, October 8.

The house itself was off limits because it was destroyed, but we made our way to the backyard. For the first time since the fighting began, our commanders insisted that we sleep. Until morning, which was coming in a mere few hours, we were commanded to rest, refuel, and prepare for what might come next. At any given time, several soldiers from my company had to move to the front of the house closest to the kibbutz's fence and protect it, just as we had been doing the last hour. Everyone else was told to rest. Those guarding would be rotated so everyone would have a chance to lie down and close their eyes.

Finding a grassy spot in the backyard, and with the sounds of war still around me, I fell asleep in an instant. Human needs are natural, and when one gets tired, it isn't hard to get some sleep, despite the circumstances. At a certain point I was woken up, went to guard, and then returned to sleep. That was the cycle.

Two hours later, when morning came, the atmosphere in our team calmed. We made it past the night. We made it past yesterday. We didn't know what today would bring, but we hoped, at the very least, October 8 wouldn't be like October 7.

CHAPTER 7

STILL IN BE'ERI

Kibbutz Be'eri, October 8–9, 2023

Sitting on the far side of the house, farthest from the fence, I suddenly heard gunfire. Bullets were coming our way, hitting the home. Terrorists in the open field, probably noticing an IDF presence around this particular house, started shooting toward us. Behind the house, I felt safe, but I had friends in front, on their guard shifts, who were more exposed. They responded. Unable to find the exact location of the terrorists, they shot in the direction of the gunfire. After several moments, though, while still not being able to spot the terrorists, and with no more bullets coming our way, we gave up. The terrorists must have been far away, and there were trees and bushes in the distance to get behind. Nonetheless, this moment showed us one thing: The madness hadn't ended on October 7; a threat still loomed.

But October 8, while still intense, was nothing like the previous day and, frankly, moved slowly. The major difference, naturally, was how much we outnumbered the enemy. While the previous day was about responding to the scene, rescuing families, and fighting many terrorists,

October 8 was about a huge IDF presence dealing with the remaining terrorists, a much easier and more manageable situation. Furthermore, and most importantly, all the families had been taken far away from Be'eri, and the only civilians left were the remains of those who were killed by Hamas.

That morning, we received, for the first time, an official replenishment of supplies from the IDF. A fortified vehicle came to our area and dropped off boxes of food and equipment. We took food, drank water, and stocked up on new equipment. The area was chaotic, and there was no one controlling the scene. But, it was important we had everything we needed, and issues would be dealt with later. That, at least, was the mindset.

Our commander then gathered us in the area where we'd slept the night before or, more truthfully, those two hours. He commended us on our work but warned us that it was far from over. He mentioned, maybe even prematurely, that he expected us to finish up here and then, either that night or in the next few days, enter Gaza on the offensive. He was right, as we all understood that an offensive on Gaza was certainly on the horizon. He was off, though, by how long it would take for us to enter. It wouldn't be a few days but rather many weeks. Nonetheless, at that moment, the focus was on Be'eri, and there was still plenty of work to do.

The fighting took place, in almost its entirety, in the back of the kibbutz, farthest from the front gate. Two neighborhoods sat side by side with a main road in the middle, and from these two places came a majority of the damage, murders, and kidnappings. Throughout the morning my team stayed on one side of the road, in the neighborhood closer to the center of the kibbutz. However, by midmorning, we crossed the road, relocating to another house in the second neighborhood.

The road itself was the most dangerous because it was exposed, with no place to hide. If a terrorist was hiding in a house in the area, a soldier in the middle of the road would be a perfect target. Therefore, we crossed quickly.

Arriving at this specific house, we saw it in ruins. Tables flipped up, couches destroyed, household items thrown all over the floor; the house was a mess. However, there was something missing here; there was no blood, no awful smell. I didn't realize it immediately, but it became clear later on.

This house would be our base for much of the day and into the night. It had a main floor with a kitchen, a living space, and several bedrooms, then an upstairs, with a porch that looked south and in the direction of most of this neighborhood. In the kitchen we found gold. Oh, not literal gold, but jars of chocolate that were not only much appreciated but delicious and so became our snack throughout the day.

Our team split up into several squads, each one setting up guard shifts at three different places, facing three different directions. The goal was to protect ourselves and watch out for terrorists.

Months later, a commander of mine showed us a video of Ella Ben Ami, daughter of Ohad and Raz Ben Ami. Ella became a nationwide advocate for the hostages, fighting for her parents' release. After her mother was returned home in November 2023, she continued to fight for the release of her father, who came home after sixteen months in captivity. A famous television clip shows Ella breaking the news of their capture to Danny Kushmaro, the host of N12 News. She tells him that her father has been taken hostage, and when Danny inquires how she knows this, she responds that she saw a picture of him in Gaza. This is how the news of her parents' abduction was broken to the country and became a clip shown over and over again.

My commander showed us a video of Ella visiting her parents' house in Be'eri, what it looked like before October 7th and after.

Looking at this video, he said, "Recognize it?"

"Of course," I said, "we were there."

This house was the one in which we spent most of October 8 and into the night. Still, the question remained, why this house?

It was clear that this area of Be'eri, in the neighborhood farthest from the front gate, was hit the hardest. Many of the homes had dead bodies inside, still in their pajamas from the night before. We weren't going to position ourselves inside a home with blood and bodies and the stench of death. The home of the Ben Amis, where a different tragedy took place, was where we positioned ourselves. One day earlier, Ohad was dragged out of his home in his underwear; the next day, we were stationed in his home. Of course, I didn't know any of this at the time. The goal now was to continue the mission: Clear Be'eri of Hamas.

The day consisted of several terrorist encounters by different teams. Thankfully, for me, there was never too much danger. By the midafternoon, the scene in Be'eri seemed pretty quiet, and there was a feeling in the air that the last terrorists might have been eliminated. We were asked to pack the surplus of supplies brought to us that morning into a vehicle, essentially cleaning up the yard. As we were doing that, once again, there was gunfire.

Bullets came flying our way from down the road; the entire IDF presence was taken by surprise. We ducked down, ran for cover, and once again, were on high alert. While earlier encounters with terrorists were more orderly, this was anything but. Soldiers started running forward toward the fire. I stayed one line back, advancing forward as the front line advanced farther. At one point someone yelled, "The terrorist is wearing an IDF uniform."

In a state built on its military, many homes had an IDF uniform in their closets. For a terrorist to find one in Be'eri wasn't hard, and this tactic just added to our already complicated situation.

Eventually, the terrorist was eliminated, but not without a heavy cost. A soldier in my company, advancing forward, was accidentally shot by another IDF soldier. Although he was evacuated immediately, his situation was dire. His life, thankfully, was saved, but not without a price. His leg had to be amputated, and he would never be able to walk as he once had.

This tragic situation showed us several things. First, that as much as each terrorist deserves their day in hell, our lives were more important than their deaths. This idea was at the top of our minds in Gaza, especially as we prioritized protecting ourselves. If there were civilians to save, that was one thing, but when there weren't, our lives and our well-being needed to be the priority.

This situation also proved, once again, the responsibility we have in deciding to use our weapons. I explained earlier the significance of accidentally making the wrong decision, and every time we put our fingers on the trigger, we had to be sure we were targeting the right person.

This brings me to my last point and final takeaway from this situation. Hamas, this time, hadn't infiltrated our borders by pretending to be civilians; they'd tried impersonating one of us, the IDF soldiers. Their tactics knew no bounds, proving once again the level Hamas would go to in order to take innocent lives.

As the day went on, nothing significant happened. At one point I saw someone with a phone, so I asked him for a news update. It had been about a day since I'd last heard anything. He told me that all of Israel was watching us. *Be'eri is the epicenter*, he told me. While other areas were the focus the previous day, by this point on Sunday evening, Be'eri was the last major fight.

I knew that if all of Israel was watching us, it meant the entire Jewish people and, quite frankly, the world was watching us, too. To know that at this critical moment in Israel's existence, I was at the epicenter of defending her, gave me a sense of pride. Getting to be a part of

rescuing these families and eliminating this threat to Israel was impact-
ful. He didn't tell me much else that was happening in the news, but
that was okay.

Moments later, we were asked to do something, and it might have
been the only thing in the army, ever, that I flatly refused. Not because I
disagreed, but because of how disgusting it was. In one of the neighborhoods along the major road, there were many dead bodies of terrorists
scattered around. We were asked to pick up the bodies, move them
toward the road, and put them in piles so they would be easier to collect.
Don't worry, we were given gloves. But I couldn't do it.

I watched as my commander dragged a body by himself, and as
the insides of this terrorist scraped the concrete sidewalk, a streak of
blood was left behind. I wasn't the only one who sat on the sidelines, but
watching might have been just as bad as participating.

That night, we went to bed in the same house we were in earlier,
that of the Ben Amis. We alternated guarding throughout the night
and closing our eyes in between. The night passed in relative quiet, and
we expected that not only was the worst behind us, but that no terrorists remained.

As the sun rose on Monday, October 9, there was a sense of calm in
Be'eri. The kibbutz was filled with security personnel from the IDF,
police, and other parts of the security establishment in Israel. It wasn't
confirmed that this community was Hamas-free, but if there were any
last terrorists, they were surely outnumbered.

Suddenly, in a house nearby, a terrorist was spotted; everyone was
on high alert again. The tank by our side got into position, and after a
warning was given to everyone around us, the tank unleashed a deadly

blow to the house. Other soldiers, after the blast, went to confirm this terrorist was no longer alive. It would turn out that this was the last terrorist to be eliminated in Kibbutz Be'eri. It had taken just over two days to clear Be'eri of Hamas.

But we didn't know this at the time. For all we knew, there were other terrorists hiding throughout the kibbutz. With that in mind, our task for the day was to search Be'eri and make sure that nobody was left. That task wasn't given just to our team or company but rather to the entire IDF presence there that day.

Our team was given a strip of houses to check along the main area where the intense fighting had taken place over the previous few days. From these houses there were families killed, hostages taken, and homes destroyed. In every house we checked every room; in every room we checked every nook and cranny. From under the beds to in the closets and the bathrooms, we cleared each house with precision. It was our responsibility to search each one of our assigned houses; if every team did their job correctly, we'd be able to confirm that Be'eri was clear.

Throughout the day there were several things that stood out. By our sides were members of Zaka, the organization responsible for clearing dead bodies from the kibbutz, covering them, and taking them away for proper burial. As we cleared homes along the main strip of Be'eri where a lot of the fighting took place, Zaka was entering homes, retrieving dead Jewish bodies, and lining them on the street. As the day went on, the line got longer. Each in a body bag, massacred Jews lay on that road, and the visual was disturbing.

Going from home to home, I found something remarkable. Be'eri, as with many of the communities along the Gaza border, was relatively left-leaning politically. During the Oslo peace process, these communities became huge proponents of the collaboration and talks with Yasser Arafat and the Palestine Liberation Organization. Here, in one home in Be'eri, destroyed beyond belief, I found an action figure replica of Yitzhak Rabin shaking the hand of Arafat on September 13, 1993. This iconic moment was one of great significance. Many Israelis considered Rabin to be a traitor after that moment, and he was assassinated by an Israeli ultranationalist at the end of a rally in November 1995. An action figure like this would be hard to find in most Israeli homes.

For me, however, this moment symbolized everything. This was a community that believed in peace more than communities anywhere else. Members of Be'eri drove to the Gaza border, picked up Gazans, and drove them to work. They advocated for a shared future, and while other Israelis vehemently rejected the very idea of a Palestinian state, members of this community believed there one day could be one. Whether you agree or disagree with these Israelis, the point was clear. Of all people for this to happen to, it felt especially unjust that it was a community that believed in peace with their neighbors. In a home with an action figure of Arafat shaking the hand of Rabin, there took place a pogrom like that in Europe in the early twentieth century.

Going house to house in Be'eri, we also did something I am not too proud of, though I knew it would be accepted by every family who lived in these homes. Be'eri felt like an apocalyptic state, as if the world was ending. Homes were no longer homes, a community no longer breathing. In these homes, it was understood that whatever we found that would benefit us in some way we would take. It was not only necessary but expected that we do so.

For example, my commander carried what is called an *olar*, or a phone-like device showing a detailed map of different regions in Israel, including Be'eri. This device was super helpful in Gaza too, showing every building and structure. The *olar* needs to be charged, and just like a phone, a portable charger can provide it with a full battery. We were instructed by our commander, if we found a portable charger in a home, to give it to him. While this could be considered stealing, the owners of that portable charger would expect us to take it.

Homes were either completely destroyed or in pretty bad condition, and the owners wouldn't be expecting to get them back. We found food and ate it. Snacking in different homes became not only routine, but an internal competition. We would say that one home had better snacks than another. Why? Just because.

When the plumbing finally returned and water came out of the faucets, we were beyond appreciative. Not having changed shirts in two days and with an itch forming on my back, I took off my vest and shirt, leaned into the shower, and washed the upper half of my body. Then, finding some anti-itch cream and baby powder in the home, I applied generously. I found a dri-FIT shirt and, seeing how sweaty and gross my uniform shirt was, I knew that was necessary. With this dri-FIT shirt under my uniform, I felt more comfortable than I had since the war broke out. All of this is to say that in any other situation, one would never rummage through another home finding whatever they needed. In this situation, it was the norm.

As we went to bed on Monday night, there was an understanding that in this massacred town, with death and the stench of dead bodies everywhere, the worst was thankfully behind us. We had just finished three intense days of fighting to save the community of Be'eri and its people and had spent all of Monday searching every house, every room, under every bed, and in every closet for every last terrorist. By late afternoon on Monday, October 9, Be'eri was finally truly declared Hamas-free, and it was confirmed that the last of the terrorists had been eliminated that very morning.

Nonetheless, with Israel's security still uncertain, every community in the Gaza region remained a potential threat. For days, weeks, and months afterward, soldiers would guard each kibbutz-turned-graveyard from within and without, gradually reducing the level of emergency and the number of troops stationed in each place.

On Monday night, my team entered a house along the northern fence of Be'eri. Our objective was to keep several pairs of eyes and guns trained on the fence in case a terrorist was hiding in the surrounding fields. While my team covered one section of the border, troops from across the IDF were stationed at various points along the perimeter, ensuring there were no blind spots around the kibbutz.

We split into two groups, with half of us staying downstairs and the other half—including me—heading upstairs. Each group had its own specific section of the fence to guard, and within our group of six upstairs, the guard shifts rotated. Our commander wanted two of us on watch at a time. Two people could help keep each other awake, and if one dozed off, the other could wake him up. Two sets of eyes could also catch something one might miss. This setup meant we worked on a 1:2 schedule: one hour on guard, followed by two hours of rest. Another hour awake and alert, then another two trying to get some shut-eye. One hour struggling to stay awake, and then two hours struggling to fall back asleep—you get the idea.

Entering this house in Be'eri felt like a small luxury. The house was in relatively good condition compared to many others, and the electricity had been restored earlier that day. That small miracle meant the world to us. We turned on the air conditioning and bathed in the cold air. For anyone who has experienced Israel's hot weather, the relief of a functioning *mazgan* (air conditioner) is unparalleled. October in Israel isn't the hottest month, but it's still plenty warm. That night, after three days of grueling heat, the cool air felt like pure bliss.

But something even more meaningful than air conditioning awaited us. This house, in all likelihood, belonged to older folks. It was obvious from the furniture, the decor, and most notably, the absence of a television. Instead, we found a radio with a cord to plug into the wall. Later, in Gaza, we'd learn the critical importance of battery-powered radios as our only connection to the outside world. But on this night, with electricity restored, we plugged the radio in, heard music, and turned the dial.

Until that moment, our understanding of what was happening in Israel was limited to what we saw firsthand and word of mouth from others. I heard several updates from different people, but I hadn't listened to the news itself. As we tuned the radio to a news station, I felt like I'd been transported to another era. I imagined myself in an Israel of decades past, during the major wars of its early years. I pictured soldiers on the battlefield with a crackly radio, desperately seeking a connection to civilization. I thought of soldiers on the Golan Heights during the Yom Kippur War. But I didn't need to imagine it—this was our reality as well.

For the first time, we listened to the news from an official source, one that was broadcasting to the entire world what we had seen with our own eyes. We knew that Kibbutz Be'eri was hit harder than most, but we also knew the Hamas attack wasn't confined to one place. Even so, we hadn't yet grasped the full scale of the tragedy. As we listened, the broadcaster began sharing numbers: the known dead, the injured, and the hostages taken. She listed the communities affected and those evacuated. Then, in a somber tone, she announced, "We can now share the names of additional individuals confirmed to have been taken from this world." She began reading the names, each followed by *Z"L* (an abbreviation meaning "of blessed memory" in Hebrew).

One of my friends couldn't take it anymore. "I can't listen to this," he said and asked us to switch to music or turn off the radio completely. We respected his request and turned it off. But my curiosity got the better of me. Later, when he went out for his guard shift, I quietly turned the radio back on. I needed to know what was happening.

The station had nothing new to report. The entire broadcast was dedicated to listing the names of murdered Israelis. Eventually, I couldn't listen anymore either. I turned it off and went to bed, waking up several times during the night for my guard shifts. By morning, our three-day mission in Be'eri was ending, and we were preparing for the next stage of our war.

CHAPTER 8

THE IN-BETWEEN PERIOD

*Kibbutz Alumim and Paratrooper Training Base,
October 10–November 3, 2023*

The next stage of the war was not the sexiest. It didn't involve guns and terrorists and action-packed, movie-like scenes. The next few weeks, in what I like to call the in-between period, the time between fighting in Be'eri and fighting in Gaza, was physically draining and mentally the most difficult.

This period began on Tuesday morning, October 10, in Be'eri. Gathering our equipment, we made our way outside the kibbutz's gates. I wouldn't return for months, until I finished my IDF service. (In March 2024, a week after turning in my gun and uniform, I returned to Be'eri for a visit.) Walking outside the kibbutz gates, we loaded on buses, were given sandwiches for breakfast, and traveled down the road to a place all too familiar. Several days earlier, my October 7th story had begun across from Kibbutz Alumim, where my helicopter was shot, where I escaped onto an open battlefield and felt bullets and rockets coming my way.

Several days earlier, we had walked from Kibbutz Alumim to Be'eri;

this time we went by bus. Arriving, we understood for the first time that we could really breathe, lower our sense of alertness, and relax just a bit. For the next few days, Kibbutz Alumim would belong to my battalion. Just as we had the previous night in Be'eri, where we guarded its borders, our battalion's job for the next several days was to protect Alumim. At any given time, half of the battalion would position itself along the kibbutz's perimeter, guarding it, and the other half would reside in the middle of the kibbutz with time to relax. With the country still on high alert and terrorists still potentially loose in Israel, guarding every community in the region was an absolute must.

Arriving in Alumim on Tuesday morning, the two companies in my battalion that had been there since Saturday took charge of guarding first. This meant that my company had a chance, finally, to rest. After putting down our equipment, we had some time to ourselves. My first order of business was to find a phone and, if I could, try to get in touch with my parents.

A friend of mine had his phone and was able to briefly speak with his parents. He told me that his parents would call mine and we'd connect to each other through the phone. Several moments later, at what must have been 3:00 a.m. in New York, I spoke to my parents. While my parents had picked up details about me from other individuals through the previous days, this was the first time they'd heard from me directly, the first time they'd heard my voice. For all of us, this was something special.

I didn't have much to say. With only a few minutes, I didn't want to start getting into Be'eri and the helicopter and all the dead bodies. I told them I was okay, that everything would be okay, and that I loved them. That was it. I would next speak to my parents a few days later.

One of the goals during our time in Alumim, aside from protecting its borders, was to clean and reorganize our equipment after several days of fighting. Just like the previous week—when we prepared for a war exercise—we now did the same for our eventual entrance into Gaza.

Throughout Tuesday, October 10, I cleaned my gun, restocked on ammunition, swapped equipment that was either broken or in need of replacement, and made sure that everything I had was exactly what I would want for battle. My mindset, understandably, was different. This time we weren't preparing for a war simulation that would end in a few days, but rather for a war that could last an extended period of time. I wanted my equipment to be the best of the best.

Coming to Alumim, and finally having a chance to relax, I noticed among my friends two trends that were both comical and logical. On the morning of October 10, friends who weren't religious were suddenly putting on *tefillin*—small black leather boxes with leather straps containing scrolls of parchment inscribed with verses from the Torah—and others who'd never smoked a day in their lives were holding a cigarette between their two fingers. This simple visual perfectly embodies the feelings and atmosphere of the IDF and the country.

I found this all pretty funny, not because it didn't make sense, but because of who was doing what. Friends who joked about the Jewish religion and flouted the different non-kosher foods they'd eaten were now feeling so connected to the country and the people supporting them and praying for them. With *tefillin* around their arms and saying the Shema prayer, it was clear that they were just happy to be alive and maybe needed some extra faith to keep them safe as the war progressed. Many of these friends would lay *tefillin* every morning throughout our time in Gaza.

The smoking thing was a bit less meaningful to witness, but once again, it made sense. While I have never smoked a cigarette and never plan to, I know the act of doing so can be relaxing, or so I've been told. In a highly stressful situation, a little stress reliever is exactly what some people need. The funny thing is that some people I saw smoking I had never seen with a cigarette in their hand before, and many of them continued smoking a lot throughout Gaza. Just in these first few days after the tragedy of October 7th, I was able to see where fellow soldiers' minds were and how some coped with the stress of the day.

As I mentioned earlier, our time in Alumim had a double focus: guard the kibbutz and prepare for Gaza. I spent many hours sitting in a chair overlooking the fence. These guard shifts were relatively relaxing, and while the threat of terrorists in the area diminished as the days went on, the importance of our guard duty remained.

In between guard shifts, we found a lot of time to rest. We had lessons on first aid and evacuating wounded soldiers, on my Negev gun, and on how our team and company would operate in Gaza. Additionally, we had meetings as a team and a company with the sole purpose of debriefing and reflecting on the moment, getting a chance to discuss how we were processing the past week, certainly the craziest of our lives. In one of those meetings, I stressed to my team the importance of our safety. Everyone wants to be the hero and eliminate that terrorist, and in Be'eri I saw many instances where soldiers tried to do that. I made sure to stress that, as I said before, our lives were more important than the terrorists' deaths. They would be eliminated eventually, but *if* something happened to one of us, the rest of us would never be able to live that down. I think my team understood my point and were very receptive.

The days in Alumim had their ups and downs, but they all culminated with Shabbat that Friday night, October 13. Right beforehand, our commanders wanted all of us to speak with our families, and while we didn't have our personal phones, there were many people on the kibbutz who did. I found someone, asked if I could borrow their phone, and called my family.

For the first time since the war began, I was *really* able to speak with my parents. Unlike a few days prior, when I said only several sentences, this time I had a full-on conversation that lasted almost twenty minutes. I went a little deeper into the events of October 7th, though still just barely scratching the surface. Instead, I wanted to ask how everything was at home. On this phone call, my parents told me that they created a group chat for the sole purpose of giving updates about me. And…there were over four hundred people on the chat. I simply couldn't believe it. I couldn't imagine a group chat for the sole purpose of giving updates about my well-being, let alone that the chat had grown to over four hundred people. At its peak there were nearly six hundred members, truly something special.

After I finished my conversation with my parents, we prepared for the most special day of the week. That night at Kabbalat Shabbat services there was something palpable in the air. Going through the service, it was clear that we wanted this to feel special, to be a different Shabbat than the one from the prior week. My friends were praying with such passion, dancing and celebrating together. The Friday night before we'd all danced with Torahs on Simchat Torah; now we were dancing at Kabbalat Shabbat. Later that night, at Shabbat dinner, we ate as a battalion and enjoyed one another's company. Friday night is always my favorite night of the week, but this one was special, and rightfully so.

After more than a week in the Gaza Envelope, between Kibbutz Be'eri and Alumim, my battalion transitioned to a training schedule, preparing for our expected operation inside the Gaza Strip. From October 15 through November 4, we were located on Bach Tzanhanim, the main training base for the Paratrooper Brigade. My eight months of training before I received my red beret and officially became a combat soldier all happened here. This is where I learned to shoot, learned to fight, where I spent many weeks in the field. It's the place where eager and excited new soldiers are met with the reality and hardships of the IDF. It's a place with some of my first, yet darkest memories of my service. It's a place where everything is timed, and if one doesn't manage to complete a task in time, a punishment is coming. We came back to this base as seasoned soldiers, preparing for a war. Therefore, we had better conditions than the new recruits…well, sort of.

Since there wasn't enough room on base for our battalion, we were pushed outside of the base fence and stayed in huge white tents. There were no bathrooms, only porta-potties, and the showers rarely had hot water. There was no air conditioning during the day, or heat at night. However, I didn't really care.

Day after day, for the span of three weeks, we would leave base, travel somewhere else to train, and then come back to base in the evening. We made our way to many different areas throughout the country, including a nearly finished new apartment building in Be'er Sheva, where we practiced taking over a high-rise, just like one we might encounter in Gaza City. We spent many days in the southern base of Tze'elim, where "Mini Gaza" was built, a replica of a small Arab village used entirely for IDF forces to train.

We never knew when we'd enter Gaza, and if our top commanders and officers had any idea, they wouldn't let us know. I think, in all honesty, the idea was to always keep us ready. We could enter Gaza any day and therefore had to be prepared every day. Furthermore, it could be that in the span of a day our battalion was given a mission to enter Gaza, and once that happened there could be no dillydallying.

In addition to our war preparations, we were given one hour of phone time each evening. In most cases, active soldiers didn't face many restrictions on phone use, and it was only new recruits who were limited to one hour a day. However, due to the situation at hand—and because we were intensely training for Gaza—our phone access was heavily restricted.

Every evening, I opened my phone to an overwhelming number of messages, so many that I couldn't even begin to respond. I called my siblings and grandparents from time to time, and I spoke with my parents every night.

During these nightly calls, the layers of my October 7th story slowly began to unfold. Each night, I shared more and more of what had happened. Only after several days did I even mention that I fought in Be'eri. A few days after that, my dad asked me about the helicopter—whether that was *my* helicopter that had been shot down. And as the calls continued, I slowly learned more about what had taken place across the country. I only knew what I had seen in front of me—the bigger picture remained foreign and unknown. In fact, several weeks after the attack, my sister mentioned the Nova music festival, and I had no idea what she was referring to. We hung up, and I immediately searched the web, discovering for the first time what had happened right down the road from me. I saw videos and pictures from Nova only weeks after it took place, showing just how "in it" and yet disconnected I had been from the full scope of the war.

This period was marked by the tremendous support we received from communities and donors both in Israel and abroad. Every day, yes, *every day*, there was something. We would return from a day of training to an entire fair set up with donations for the taking. Underwear, socks, shirts, shorts, towels, thermal wear, hats, and gloves were just a few of the donations we would receive. And those were just the simple items. We received nice jackets, fleeces, military gear, protective glasses, and even a Leatherman multipurpose tool. These were quality gifts, and people's generosity was hard to believe. Every day we'd receive something, and I remember joking, "This is an army I can get behind!" and

"Where was this throughout my entire service?" I understood we were in a war and therefore received many donations, but this was excessive. I would feel as if I was in a store, but with no price tags. Anything I saw, I could take.

And the donations didn't stop there. Every night we'd come back to an elaborate meal of some sort. I don't think I ate as much steak in my life as I did the weeks leading up to Gaza. Every night there would be shawarma, or burgers, or steak, or anything you might think of. Barbecues and platters of fresh fruit, meat, chicken, and a ton of desserts. We couldn't believe the donations brought to us, and for the first time in my nearly two years of serving, I couldn't recognize the IDF. This wasn't the army I knew, but I understood this was an anomaly due to the seriousness of this war. I knew this wouldn't last forever, as we were about to enter Gaza, but I decided to enjoy it for the time being.

Mentally, however, this period was by far the hardest of the war. When one is in something, as we were when in the combat zone of Be'eri, one doesn't have much time to think. It's only when one steps away, has time to think and hear their thoughts, that one starts thinking about everything that happened and is yet to happen.

After October 7th and before Gaza, several soldiers in my company either dropped out or there was a mutual decision between them and their commanders that it was best they didn't continue. After everything we saw and experienced in a real and intense combat zone, the fact that some people couldn't continue is completely understandable. Two people in my company, for example, after the helicopter incident, were already in bad enough condition that they didn't even enter Kibbutz Be'eri, which happened within two hours of one another. Others decided right when we arrived at our training base that they couldn't continue. However, I think the hardest were those who stuck with it and, over the span of a few weeks, their condition worsened.

Like I said, this period between October 7th and Gaza gave us all time to think: to think about what Gaza would look like, if it would be as dangerous as Kibbutz Be'eri, and to think about all of the "what ifs." *What if something happens to me? What if I am killed, or seriously injured? What if my friend is killed? What about my family back home? My parents? My siblings?*

I think these questions caused several to really panic. Some people, understandably so, after everything we saw on October 7th, weren't ready for Gaza, and it was therefore decided they wouldn't continue as a combat soldier in this war.

While I never reached that extreme, the unknown was scary. I would tell myself that I knew what fighting looked like. I saw fighting on October 7th, and I was aware of it now, something I didn't know a few weeks prior. However, I didn't know what Gaza would look like. Would it look like October 7th? Would there be different dangers in Gaza that we didn't have to deal with in Kibbutz Be'eri? Had I done enough to prepare, or was there more I must do? I knew what happened on October 7th, and I thought to myself, if every day in Gaza looked like that, I wasn't capable. And if something happened to me, would I regret not backing out now?

I had these thoughts, in all honesty, but they were minimized by my goals and the reassurances we received from our commanders. First of all, they would reassure us that Gaza wouldn't look like the fighting on October 7th. Unfortunately, Israel wasn't ready on October 7th, and we were on the defensive. These commanders reassured us that in Gaza we would be in control. Every operation would be conducted methodically, with a plan and with precision. There would be mistakes, but the IDF would be in control. Furthermore, they would tell us that during the October 7th attack the IDF had used only a small fraction of its power. Most of the fighting was our guns versus their guns, our battalion commander would say. However, in Gaza we were about to see the full force of the IDF, with its Air Force, Navy, artillery, tanks, technology, and finally us, the simple infantry soldiers. Our battalion commander made it clear that he wouldn't send us into any dangerous situation if he didn't have to and that he'd prefer to use air strikes or tanks rather than an infantry soldier with only his gun. This, we would learn upon entering Gaza, was exactly what happened and helped save our lives countless times.

In addition to these reassurances, my mindset and determination pushed me forward. As hard as it was to be a soldier post–October 7th and before entering Gaza, I knew that this was what I had signed up for. Years earlier, when I decided to enlist in the IDF, I knew that if there was a war, I would be there to fight. This wasn't because I'd want to, but rather because this was the job. In a two-year service, it was my "luck" that war broke out with fewer than three months of my service to go, but I knew there was no backing out. I was not backing out just when the time had come that I was needed. And most of our service was built around training for a war, in case one came. We don't train to stand guard in Hebron or to go on some sort of arrest in Ramallah. Our training was focused on war and how to react if and when one comes. This war came, and this is what I had been preparing for from the moment I put on my uniform.

The last reason pushing me through was the hostages, especially my friend Omer. When we arrived at Bach Tzanhanim on October 15, we were given an hour on our phones, and I called my family. This wasn't the first time I'd spoken with them, but this was the first time speaking with them on my personal phone. It was during this call that my parents told me about Omer. They said that they had been hiding Omer's kidnapping from me since it happened because they didn't want me to stress any more than I had to, after everything I'd already gone through. However, now that I was on my own phone, they didn't want me finding out on my own about Omer's kidnapping. My parents told me that it had been confirmed that Omer was one of the hostages, that he was taken from his tank serving along the Gaza border that morning. I was in utter shock. I hung up the phone and took a moment for myself.

Thinking about Omer and the other hostages, I knew that I had to continue and do what I could for their release. There was a feeling in the air among every Jew worldwide that they had to do something. Whether that was donating, attending rallies, or speaking up for the hostages, there was a sense of responsibility. I felt lucky enough to be in the IDF at this specific time and have the chance to fight for Omer's return. I thought about him every day. I thought about what he must be going through, what the hostages were all going through. I couldn't sit back. No matter how hard it was to be a soldier entering Gaza, I knew I had to fight for him and everyone else taken by the evil terrorists that October morning.

This period culminated in a special visit, days before finally entering Gaza. Since we were nearly a month straight in the army, with no breaks at home, there was one thing on everyone's minds: family. It had been almost a month since we had seen our loved ones, and this clearly wasn't just any month. It was a month where we saw our lives flash in front of our own eyes, and our people suffered the biggest blow we could never have expected.

Granting us several days at home, days before entering Gaza, wasn't on the table, so the decision was made to bring home to the base. We were given half a day where parents, siblings, aunts, uncles, cousins, friends, and anyone close to us could visit. Outside our base, cars parked with baskets of homemade food and desserts, all brought by friends and family members to spoil their loved ones, their soldiers, tell them how much they loved them, and give them some motivation before they entered Gaza. The issue for me, of course, was that my family wasn't there.

The problem always, for a Lone Soldier, is a lack of family. When everyone goes home on a normal weekend, they are welcomed back to the home they grew up in, go to sleep in the same bed they know. This time I was lucky. On that day, when hundreds of families from across Israel gathered outside the Bach Tzanhanim base, my host mother, Geula, from Kibbutz Erez, and my coordinator from Garin Tzabar, Talia, came for a visit. They brought food, sat with me for a while, and gave me the attention I not only loved but also needed at that moment.

However, I was much luckier than just that. Months earlier, way before October 7th meant anything to the world, my parents had booked tickets to visit Israel at the end of October. Now, even with the war ongoing, my parents still decided to come. They boarded a flight without even knowing if they'd get to see me. Unfortunately, though, my parents arrived a day after everyone's families were allowed to visit.

I begged my commander to let me see my family the next day, on Shabbat. While no one else was receiving additional family time, my commander understood my special predicament and granted me the privilege. The next day, while my friends stayed on base, continuing to prepare for Gaza, I left for several hours as my parents traveled all the way to my base. Sitting outside, I saw them for the first time since the war began, and we sat for hours in conversation. Talking about home, talking about the war, and talking about life. That afternoon was special, and I understood more than ever how much my family, friends, and community back in New York were thinking about me. All of this gave me the strength to move on.

After weeks of training for Gaza, each day believing it would be our last one on base, the day we were waiting for finally came. On November 4, 2023, we woke up to the news that today was the day. We were told to gather our equipment and finish up final details. The night before, I was able to speak to my family, and while I didn't know at the moment that I'd enter Gaza the next day, I knew they'd somehow find out.

That morning, I put the final touches on all my equipment. It was most important, however, that I had food and a lot of it. Going through my food bag, I made sure that I had plenty of extras in case there was a delay in supplies reaching us. I also took my gun and cleaned it yet again. Did it need an extra cleaning? Probably not. But I wanted to make sure that everything I did was to be safe rather than sorry.

With all my equipment ready, I wanted to do one last thing. I took one of the pocket *siddurim* (prayer books) donated to our battalion and put it in my pocket. I then decided to write a note. I've heard of soldiers heading into war writing notes to their families in case something happened. This idea made me somewhat emotional, and I thought a lot about whether to do so, but in the end decided to pick up a pen and write. With my note in hand, I took the *siddur* out of my pocket, opened it to the page of the Shema, folded my note in half, and placed it on that page. Closing the *siddur*, I put it once again in my pocket.

But doing this last act before heading into Gaza was one that troubled me, and not because I didn't know what to write, but rather because I didn't know if I should have written it at all. Several weeks later, after leaving Gaza for the first time, I decided to take out my note and burn it. Superstitiously, I felt that I had written my own death note, and I didn't want to bring on anything bad. My rationale was that if something, G-d forbid, happened to me, my family would know how much I'd miss them, and I didn't need a note to tell them. A letter in case I died was just putting bad omens into the air.

Nonetheless, on November 4, I had that note and the *siddur* in my pocket, a bag full of equipment, and a gun as clean as I could get it. This time was for real. While there were other days over the past few weeks when we thought we were going in, this time felt different, and it was different. Making our way to the pickup zone, we loaded onto buses and headed west toward the Gaza Envelope. The in-between period was coming to an end, and the next chapter of the war was beginning.

CHAPTER 9

ENTERING GAZA

Gaza Border, November 4–5, 2023

All of our preparations brought us to the Shokeda Forest, nestled between the communities of Shokeda and Be'eri. Here, under the trees and sitting on the dirt, we waited until evening before finally entering Gaza. We put final touches on our equipment, sprayed oil in our guns, and made sure we were ready to go.

Sitting next to a commander of mine and two others, we discussed expectations upon entering Gaza, as this was our first time crossing the border. Despite all the stories we heard from Operation Protective Edge in 2014, the last time the IDF entered Gaza by foot, and despite fighting in Kibbutz Be'eri, we knew this would be different.

We sat and waited in this forest for several hours. In the IDF, waiting for anything is common, and this could be said about waiting for a bus, a meal to begin, or even entering the Gaza Strip. The idea of waiting became something to get used to, and this just gave us opportunities to be creative or, in this case, talk amongst ourselves.

As the conversation continued, my commander asked us to share one thing we wanted to accomplish in Gaza or, in simpler terms, a goal or dream of ours. He wasn't referring to a shared goal of the IDF, or a shared goal of our platoon or team. Rather, he asked us, "What is that one thing you are imagining in your mind, that one thing you have played over and over in your head? What is that personal heroic moment of yours that you've thought about over these last few weeks, that you wish to achieve, no matter how feasible or realistic it is?"

This question reminded me of dreaming about a huge sports game. Beyond the physical preparations leading up to the game, it is common to dream of hitting that walk-off home run or scoring that last-second goal, or hitting the buzzer-beater, three-point shot to win the game. In that same vein, my commander asked us to share what was on our minds.

My friend answered first by saying he imagined himself in a small forest, one of the many throughout Gaza, lying on the ground with his machine gun. All of a sudden, he imagined several terrorists exiting a tunnel with the intent of attacking him and our team. Before these terrorists even have a chance to grasp the situation, he eliminates them all with one spray of his machine gun and not only has he killed these terrorists but protected his guys, his friends. Other answers included finding tunnels that led to important intelligence or Hamas infrastructure, and other answers focused on the hostages. "All I want to do is find a hostage and bring him home, no matter who they are."

At this point, on November 4, 2023, nearly all of the hostages were still in Gaza.

I answered last and told my commander that for weeks, ever since October 15, when my parents told me that my friend Omer was taken hostage, I have dreamed of bringing him home. I have imagined a scenario where I identify Omer, no matter how similar or different he looks from the way I knew him, and I shout at everyone on my team to stop shooting. I take command of the situation, telling my commander there is a hostage, and describing what I saw and what he's wearing. We then quickly discuss a game plan to get him safely in our hands. I imagined a situation where he escaped from his captors and made his way to IDF forces and prayed that the IDF doesn't mistake him for a terrorist. In this situation, I hoped I would be a familiar face for Omer, and because I would be the only one on my team who knows what he looks like, I would help identify him. I knew this was unlikely to happen, but my commander reminded me that he'd asked for a dream of ours, and we could be as imaginative as we wanted.

We sat in the Shokeda Forest until evening, waiting for the vehicles to take us into Gaza. Eventually two types of vehicles arrived. The first, huge trucks that fit more than twenty-five men in each. The majority of soldiers in my battalion were taken on one of those, but I was even luckier.

In front of these big trucks came the smaller Jeeps to lead the way. These Jeeps look exactly like the ones you'd take on an off-road tour for leisure. I was told that I was lucky to be chosen to ride in a Jeep rather than a truck. After a small briefing we strapped ourselves in. As always, I made sure to empty my bladder as many times as possible before leaving the forest. There was no estimate on how long the ride would be, and I knew that once we left the forest, there wouldn't be any bathroom breaks along the journey. It's not like we could stop somewhere along the Jersey Turnpike; we were heading into Gaza, after all.

Sitting beside me in the Jeep was the other Negevist on my team. We sat side by side on the back bench of the Jeep, looking behind us. Just like on the helicopter a few weeks earlier, our bags were by our feet and there wasn't very much leg room in which to move around. In fact, there was barely any room for one person with all their equipment, and we had to fit two. Once again, a minor discomfort in a more serious situation.

As the sun was setting, we hit the road. Driving away from the forest, we left the dirt paths and made it onto the main roads in the Gaza Envelope. I looked out onto the street signs to get a feeling for where I was, and within moments, it started to hit me. Making a right turn toward a community, I realized we were heading in the same direction where we had fought weeks earlier. We drove toward the front gate of Kibbutz Be'eri. Before the entrance, we made a right turn and drove along the outside perimeter of Be'eri, with the kibbutz's fence to our left. Through the fence, I saw the roads we had walked down, the houses we were in, the spots that only weeks earlier had been littered with dead bodies, and the areas where I had fought against terrorists.

While this was the direction of the Netzarim Corridor, the main East-West path across Central Gaza, there was a greater meaning to driving past Kibbutz Be'eri. We were reminded of what happened to us just several weeks prior, and why this war started to begin with. We were reminded of the death, destruction, and hostages. Before risking our lives and heading into Gaza, we had to remember the why. Remind ourselves of our past before heading into our future.

Leaving Be'eri, we continued toward Gaza. Before crossing, we arrived at an area with IDF vehicles and tents set up right next to the border. However, the funniest thing came next. Out of a rugged-looking car, two ultra-Orthodox men came out with candy and drinks. Throwing us the candy, they said, *"Tachzeru b'shalom"*—"Come back in peace"—a common phrase said to soldiers heading into battle. All I could think of was *How in the world did they get here?!* There were no other civilians in the area aside from these two, throwing candy at any soldier they saw. While this interaction was a bit comical, it wasn't the last time it happened. Almost every time we reentered Gaza, there was a group of Orthodox Jews throwing us treats and even handing out religious books such as *siddurim* (prayer books) or *tehilim* (book of psalms). Whenever this happened, the one thing on my mind was how they had gotten there. Who would let these nonmilitary individuals get so close to the border? It always shocked me, but I decided to just enjoy the treats.

From there, we drove a bit farther, and before I knew it, we were crossing the border onto the dirt roads of Gaza. Under my breath I said the Shehecheyanu prayer because this was my first time in Gaza. Growing up, my mom would have us say this prayer for every "first," and I thought crossing into Gaza certainly warranted that prayer.

Continuing down the road, the ultimate off-road Jeep experience commenced. With dirt flying in the air and the Jeep bouncing up and down from the bumps along the road, I felt as if I was on some Jeep tour in the Arizona desert. The dirt blew in my face, and I was grateful I had my protective glasses on over my eyes. The problem, however, was my gun. It was now covered in the dirt that came from every direction. If dirt found its way inside the gun, it might affect its shooting and required a super-deep clean. As you can imagine, after spending hours cleaning my gun, I found this beyond frustrating.

We made many stops on our way into Gaza. This is relatively funny in hindsight, but it turned out there was traffic on the Netzarim Corridor. There were many tanks and other military vehicles crossing at an intersection up ahead, which meant we had to wait. We sat on that Jeep for hours into the night, but thankfully, we were allowed to get off and use the bathroom from time to time.

At a certain point we were told that we were turning around. "Turning around!" I said. "To where?" Apparently, with all the traffic on the Netzarim Corridor, there was no way the entire 890th Battalion would reach our destination by dawn. This was important because we were supposed to reach our location in the middle of the night and then go on the attack just as the sun rose. If we were to reach the location after sunrise, the entire plan would be delayed, and we would be unable to attack until the next day at sunrise. Turning around, we made our way back toward Israel, crossing the border and at around 3:00 a.m. reaching that same forest we had just left. From there, we waited another hour until buses came to take us to Kibbutz Sa'ad. There, in one of their community centers, we all were given pads to sleep on.

It would turn out that in all my days and nights in Gaza, this was one of the worst. From sitting on those Jeeps for hours into the night and then having to turn around, our morale was crushed. We finally made it into Gaza and then, just like that, we were out. In total, I had spent five hours inside the strip.

There is this concept in the IDF known as *shnei*, which literally means "two." In training, *shnei* comes up a lot, with a slightly different meaning. Whenever a commander says that one word, *shnei*, whatever you just did has to be repeated. After running a lap around a building and not finishing in the time the commander set forth, he'd wait for everyone to return, and then, building up suspense, he'd look us dead in the eyes and say, "*Shnei.*" Now, we had to run that lap again. In a less punishing sense, the word is used when we need to repeat a drill, or simply do something over.

The next day, after our unfortunate five-hour journey into Gaza, we were told *shnei*. Heading back to the Shokeda Forest, we waited for hours. Then, hopping back on the Jeeps, we drove past Kibbutz Be'eri again and headed into Gaza. This time, there was no traffic. We made our way to our destination for the night, an IDF outpost within Gaza. Throughout the war, the IDF set up central outposts throughout the strip that were away from the action and fighting, but close enough to where major forces were stationed.

The idea was to spend the night outside on the dirt in this field and then make our way to the destination of our first offensive in the morning. That night, Sunday, November 5, 2023, was my first night in Gaza. For the next several hours, I tried to sleep in between waking up several times for guard duty. The weather was cold and the sky was filled with stars. Around us was the sound of Hamas rocket fire and IDF air strikes, but nothing prevented a quick sleep from time to time throughout the night. The surrounding area was dark, and it was hard to even see several dozen meters in front of us. However, we would learn more about our location as the sun rose.

CHAPTER 10

GAZA CITY

Gaza City, November 4–December 1, 2023

As dawn came and the stars started to disappear, our surroundings became clearer. Looking out, only a few hundred meters away sat the beautiful and calm Mediterranean Sea. Hours earlier, upon arrival, I couldn't tell you we were that close, but the cold breeze throughout the night now made a whole lot more sense.

The goal of our battalion that day, my first full day in Gaza, was to take control of an area of Gaza City along the water. Currently, we were along the Netzarim Corridor near the sea, south of the city. Our journey that day would take us north.

After gathering our equipment and once our entire battalion was ready, we were off. My company led the way, and we walked a few hundred meters toward the sea, literally heading onto the sand, and then, from there, we trekked north. It would turn out that during my entire four months in Gaza, this would be one of the hardest things I'd do physically. For the next two kilometers we walked on the Gaza beach. With the sun shining, the cold overnight turned to a strong heat, and walking on sand made the trek all the more difficult. Entering into new territory, our unit had to be careful and precise with how we advanced, and this meant stopping many times along the way.

We were one of the first IDF forces to walk along the Gaza beach in decades, and the sights and feelings were something special. As I turned to my left, the Mediterranean Sea sat calmly, and to my right an intense war ensued.

Continuing north, we started to approach the beach of Gaza City, and I was a little shocked at its beauty and normalcy. Gaza is thought to be a poor place under "Israeli occupation," where the people don't have enough food, clothes, and basic goods. The scenes on that beach spoke differently.

Walking past lifeguard stands and beach lounge chairs, restaurants and different areas to sit and enjoy the view, I felt as if I was several kilometers north in Tel Aviv. Don't get me wrong, I'd always prefer an evening at Gordon Beach in Tel Aviv, but this wasn't too shabby. This was still the same Mediterranean Sea that stretched along Israel's coastline, only several kilometers south.

Finally, approaching Gaza City, we made it to the Remal neighborhood, filled with high-rise buildings, and soon I'd see for myself how nice some of these apartments were. The Remal neighborhood is known to be one of the nicer areas in the strip, and for an initial welcome to Gaza, this was certainly a treat.

What's important to remember is that this entire area of Gaza was supposed to have been cleared of civilians, though we knew it wasn't. When the decision was made for the IDF to enter Gaza, Israel made it well known and, unlike any other military, told their enemy where they would attack. Civilians were told to evacuate the area to Southern Gaza, using many methods, including radio broadcasts, direct calls, and leaflets dropped from Israeli Air Force planes. I collected a few of those leaflets, written in Arabic, with those warnings.

This was the first day of more than one hundred that I spent in the Gaza Strip. As you'll read, some days were filled with activity and even danger, while others—the majority—were spent not doing much of anything. I'll get to that later.

Our first day consisted of much of what my battalion did operationally in Gaza time and again, which was to attack, enter, clear, and secure an area. Simultaneously, we searched for terrorists; signs of their infrastructure, such as guns, missiles, tunnels, or anything that could provide intelligence or information for the IDF to use; and of course, any signs of life of our beloved hostages.

Our first such attack took place in the Remal neighborhood of Gaza City, directly across from the beach on which we just walked, across the main street in several of the apartment buildings. The goal was to take over the buildings, search for any terrorists or information they had left behind, and then live in the buildings. Essentially: enter and clear. This was my first "operational activity" in Gaza, so there was a sense of fear in my mind and the butterflies in my stomach were certainly churning.

While preparing our gear to go in, I saw the whole of the IDF at work. Moments earlier, as we were nearing Gaza City, we took a brief pause as we were awaiting an air strike from the Israeli Air Force. Suddenly, waiting on the sandy Mediterranean beach, I heard a huge boom ahead: The air strike had come. Waiting to cross the street and clear the buildings, I watched as tanks erupted and shot heavy fire toward our destinations. A friend on my team took his gun with a *matol* attached, a grenade launcher, and went to a spot to fire grenades in the same direction the tanks were firing.

As an infantry soldier, my job, with my team, is to come in last and clear the building room by room. Only with physical boots on the ground can we officially claim possession of a building, and we were the ones who did that. First came the air strikes, then the artillery, tanks, grenades, you name it. This was all done to clear out the enemy from the location, and it served as protection for the soldiers on the ground, making it as safe as possible for us to enter the buildings. This methodical approach was just as our commanders had explained in the previous days and weeks as we prepared to enter Gaza.

Waiting on the beach, I watched as the IDF and its weaponry fired from all directions. Then, with the green light, we ran. Carrying our bags, we sprinted across the street. Entering the first building, with me positioned right next to my commander, our company cleared each floor. Then, the command was given to cross a courtyard and take over the next building. Just like the first, we took our bags and ran with our weapons, always facing forward. Entering the first floor, we ascended to each level clearing the building. Neither building had any terrorists, and we performed our first operation with ease.

You might be thinking how quick that was. Two buildings? That's it? With all the hype and walking several kilometers on the beach, all we did was take over two buildings? And you'd be right. It took some time for me to get used to it, but you have to understand one important thing: My company and I cleared two buildings, and, next to us, other companies in our battalion cleared other buildings. Beyond that, other battalions and brigades cleared others. The IDF works because on the micro level we all do our job; on the macro level, everything comes into place. My company cleared two buildings in this specific offensive, but in the span of several weeks, the IDF cleared the majority of Gaza City. Each person must do their job, and then, as a whole, the IDF has done its job.

In the house we now entered, my shock and amazement at Gaza continued. This apartment was fancier than my house back home in New York. This apartment had marble floors, detailed curvatures, and, of course, a view of the Mediterranean Sea. If there wasn't a war, and Gaza wasn't controlled by a terrorist organization, I'd say this place would make for a pretty nice vacation spot. Anyway, this building became our home for the next few days. After my first day in Gaza, a long day I will never forget, I snuggled up in a corner of the house and went to sleep.

For the next several days, our unit conducted several raids and attacks with the goal of moving slowly eastward from the beach farther into Gaza City. Just to clarify: There's a difference between a raid and an attack. During a raid, we leave our current home, carry out the mission, and return when it's over. An attack means we move to a new area, take it over, and make it our new base. Not every day did we have a mission assigned. Some days in this first week we simply remained in place and waited for our next task to be assigned to us.

One day when we were not on a mission, a friend came to me and said that he heard that my mom was on the radio. Several teams in my battalion already had found radios, amazing access to the outside world.

My mom? I thought to myself. *No frickin' way my mom is on Israeli radio.* I thought he must be mistaken. The next day, though, another person came to me and said the same thing. That same day, a bit later, I heard this from a third person.

Apparently, they were correct. My mom, back on Long Island, was interviewed on Galgalatz, a major Israeli radio station, along with my host mother from Kibbutz Erez, Geula, on a segment called *Kolah Shel Ima* or *A Mother's Voice.* Together, they spoke about me, my journey in the IDF and in the war, and the relationship between our two families. Most important of all, the entire interview was done in Hebrew. My mother, while taking Ulpan online and always studying her Hebrew skills, was far from fluent, and had certainly never done anything like that before. The following month, when I was out of Gaza and had my phone, I was able to listen to a recording of the entire interview. My mother struggled with Hebrew but did great. The interview was very special because it showed the closeness of my host family in Israel and my biological family back in New York and highlighted the journeys and importance of Lone Soldiers.

Back to the war.

Beginning Wednesday, November 15, we went on operations two days in a row. We woke up, waited around throughout the morning, and around 12:30 p.m. we finally headed out on a raid. Our assignment was to take over two buildings, which we did one after the other. After securing them, we returned to the first building while other teams in our battalion took care of their targets. While we waited, a few of us, myself included, covered the direction of Al-Quds University, watching for anything suspicious. Meanwhile, others on my team conducted a deep search of the building and found several Hamas-related items, including a detailed booklet filled with intelligence Hamas had on Israel. We later learned that this was an incredible find.

After that, we were given a new task: take over another building. As we approached, we quickly realized this was no ordinary structure—it was a mansion. Easily the fanciest building we'd come across so far. It had a massive generator, and even the elevator was still working. This was a stark contrast to most of Gaza, where you couldn't find a single ounce of electricity. Given the location—so close to the heart of Gaza City and near Shifa Hospital—we soon discovered that whoever lived here was a high-ranking figure in Hamas. As is protocol for a site like this, once we finished searching and collecting intel, we destroyed the building so it could not be used for terrorist activity again.

After this we made our way back to our original position, not necessarily knowing what to expect the next day. However, it ended up being a day filled with action, fear, and, in all honesty, the first time in Gaza that I truly felt like I was in a war.

The night before, our commander woke us at around 8:45 p.m.—yes, we went to bed early in Gaza—and said that tomorrow would be a busy and intense day, possibly the first real battle our battalion would face during our time in Gaza. The next morning, our company led the way, this time advancing two kilometers eastward. Unlike the first day, when we walked on the beach mainly through territory already controlled by the IDF, this time we were moving through areas that had not yet been cleared. It was our responsibility to remain sharp and as alert as possible.

Along the way, we encountered two Gazans who clearly weren't supposed to be there, posed a threat, and were eliminated. We continued pushing forward, and as we approached our destination, we suddenly heard gunfire and several RPGs launched. We quickly took over our designated building and scanned the area from inside, trying to locate the enemy. The shooting continued, and our building provided protection. This was the first time our battalion had come under fire in Gaza.

Later, we were told to move again—this time two hundred meters closer to where the rest of the battalion was located. Under fire—mainly coming from the opposite side of the building we had just left—we threw on our heavy bags and advanced, clearing a much smaller house. Unlike many of the buildings we had stayed in before, this one was run-down. The entire area looked more like what people imagine when they think of Gaza.

That night turned out to be one of the coldest we had experienced so far. The building didn't insulate us from the cold or the sounds of explosions the way other, better-built homes had. But we were all physically and mentally drained, and everyone fell asleep quickly and deeply.

We were supposed to reach the Hamas base in the area that day, but it had gotten too late, so we were told we would try again the next day. However, when the next day came, they didn't need the entire battalion for this task. Another team in our company went on this operation, and it turned out to be pretty successful. Since this was a more tense area than we had seen up until that point, they ended up encountering some action. Our company eliminated three terrorists, with the entire battalion eliminating twenty in all.

We had a successful day ourselves, finding a small radio that only required two batteries, and this saved us tremendously. We spent the entire day huddled around that radio, listening to the news and music. It brought some much-needed normalcy into this war zone, especially because we had been disconnected from the rest of the world for about two weeks.

The next morning, we went on a small operation at around 2:00 p.m. This wasn't the longest or the craziest day yet, but because of what we found, it proved to be the most significant since entering Gaza. The goal was to take over several buildings surrounding the mosque nearby, so that Yahalom—the special forces combat engineering unit that focuses on explosives—could enter the mosque and search for a weapons storage and manufacturing site, which intelligence believed was hidden inside.

As we approached one of the surrounding buildings, we discovered a tunnel located right outside. When Yahalom entered the mosque, they found another tunnel entrance, along with other significant finds. These tunnels were too dangerous to enter on foot, and there was no reason to risk anyone's life unnecessarily, so they sent a robot with a camera into the tunnel, as is standard practice in the IDF.

As expected, the robot confirmed that the tunnel led to a weapons storage and manufacturing lab. It also revealed tunnel connections that, according to our commanders, led to Hamas's major underground metro system, connecting this location directly to their central headquarters.

Yahalom worked tirelessly for hours while we stayed in one of the surrounding buildings, taking shifts guarding and eventually getting some sleep as the night wore on. Our responsibility was to protect Yahalom while they did the interesting work. We didn't finish until around 10:30 p.m., and since there was still plenty of work to do, we were told we'd be coming back the next day so that Yahalom could continue gathering more intelligence.

The next day we woke up at 6:30, and by 7:00 we were already advancing toward the mosque, setting up guarding positions overlooking it and the surrounding area. I was guarding to the south and could see the Hamas base our battalion had taken over a few days prior. That base was right next to a school. I thought about how classic Hamas that was—placing a base next to a school. At least this time they hadn't put the base *inside* the school.

Most of the day was uneventful, as we alternated between guarding and resting. Then, at one point, my commander asked a few of us if we wanted to tour the findings underneath the mosque. I jumped at the opportunity.

Entering the mosque, it was clear that the main level was a normal prayer space. Beautiful and decorative, this mosque was exactly what it was supposed to be…a mosque. However, we then descended downstairs and saw what was directly beneath the prayer space. Yahalom had blown through certain walls in the basement to reach hidden rooms filled with Hamas's supplies, planning, weapons, and tunnel entrances. In one room, we saw a diagram on a whiteboard that detailed how they transferred weapons underground using a cart system—and then we saw the actual cart itself. Eventually, we were led into a room with the Hamas emblem on the wall. Surrounding us was a large stockpile of weapons: rockets, guns, explosive materials, and more. Most striking of all were the rockets marked with Russian lettering, showing clearly who was supplying—or at least manufacturing—some of these weapons.

The tour was beyond fascinating. It confirmed everything I had learned about Hamas using civilian infrastructure for their terrorist activities.

With 251 hostages taken and brought deep into the tunnels of Gaza, returning the hostages to their families was a major goal of our operations there. And, because the IDF operates with Jewish values, our texts shape our actions. The scripture tells us the following:

Anyone who destroys one soul from the Jewish people, the verse ascribes him as if he destroyed an entire world, and anyone who sustains one soul from the Jewish people, the verse ascribes him as if he sustained an entire world" (Mishnah Sanhedrin 4:5; Babylonian Talmud, Sanhedrin 37a).

This idea of saving life with regard to the hostages had been a central discussion within the IDF since October 7th. Whether a hostage is alive or not, bringing them home to their family and their people is of utmost importance. Locating and rescuing hostages was obviously a goal, but short of that, simply applying constant, fierce military pressure on Hamas is what we believed would, and ultimately did, bring Hamas to the negotiating table. I'm proud to say I played a role in that.

Now, by late November, almost fifty days since the horrible massacre of October 7th, a deal was in place, and for the first time since the war began, hostages began coming home. For the span of a week in late November, over one hundred hostages were brought home to Israel: women, children, and foreign workers. The deal, in the eyes of Israelis, was a favorable one. Instead of receiving one hostage for over one thousand terrorists, as was the case with Gilad Shalit (a former Israeli hostage taken by Hamas in 2006 and returned to Israel in 2011), every hostage was brought home in return for three terrorists—a good "exchange rate." Again, we knew and were proud that the military pressure we were applying was certainly a huge reason why this agreement had been made.

We spent the week of the ceasefire in Gaza along the coast with minimal responsibilities. We had to guard the area where we were, but we weren't heading out on any operations. Despite this, the week still ended up having some interesting moments.

Since Gazan civilians knew we couldn't act offensively, many returned to Northern Gaza. After almost three weeks of not seeing any civilians, the area suddenly became filled with cars, horse carriages, and people walking around. This complicated things. We had to be more alert due to the increased movement. There's a big difference between a civilian walking by and a Hamas terrorist trying to blend in. And despite the ceasefire, if Hamas were to attack us, we obviously had the right to return fire.

Civilians were allowed to move around but not get too close to our positions. At my guard post, I was told that if anyone crossed a certain road, I had permission to shoot a warning shot into a sand dune about thirty meters ahead. During my shift, I fired one warning shot. Others who guarded during more active times fired several. For our safety, it was important that we didn't allow any Gazans to come close to our post. On that same note, it was even more important we didn't do anything stupid, like shooting a Gazan civilian who was not posing a real threat, which could have put the ceasefire as a whole in jeopardy. The line between protecting ourselves while not doing anything to sabotage the deal on the table was something we had to balance.

The Shabbat during the ceasefire was one of my most special yet. Since our entire company was in one building, we gathered for an electric and meaningful Kabbalat Shabbat.

Beyond the wonderful Shabbat vibes, we received a nice treat—letters from our families. I received letters from my parents, my brother, my sister, and my host family. It was such a thoughtful surprise and definitely made my day. One of the letters mentioned a huge pro-Israel rally held in Washington, DC, and said, "I'm sure you already know about this, but we wanted to tell you anyway."

I was completely out of the loop and only had access to a radio after that rally had already taken place, so I didn't know about it. Those letters were a real morale boost.

The rest of Shabbat was spent eating a ton of food brought in for the day—mainly chocolate croissants and rugelach—and playing board games. Everyone seemed to get into the activities as a way to pass the time, and it turned into a fun way to relax. We also spent a few hours organizing and cleaning our gear, which was necessary. Everything was filled with sand, and it felt good to finally get everything clean, orderly, and back in place. We ended the day with Havdalah (a ceremony marking the end of Shabbat and the start of a new week) together as a group.

The week continued with several more exciting moments. I had the opportunity to call home for the first time since entering Gaza. We were given old Nokia flip phones and had to make them work. Due to the bad signal, I had to ascend to the top of our building, and even with that, finding a signal was tough. I ended up calling my host father from Kibbutz Erez, who connected me with my parents.

Despite the ceasefire, we continued our training and performed several drills. At one point we pretended that someone in our building was shot and then had to evacuate them on a stretcher, down six flights of stairs, and into an evacuation vehicle. At another point we went to the Gaza City beach, made a makeshift shooting range, and made sure our guns were properly calibrated. Shooting on the Gaza beach as if I was at some shooting range in the Israeli desert was truly unique.

The ceasefire was supposed to come to an end on Tuesday night, November 28, and we expected to leave Gaza for a few days before eventually coming back in, but this time to Shejaiya. That night we boarded military trucks, left our position along the coast, and started heading toward Israel. The excitement in the air was palpable as finally, after nearly a month, we were heading back. Then, along the journey, we suddenly made a U-turn. A bit surprised, we wondered why we were heading back the way we'd come. There were two reasons. First, the ceasefire was being extended, obviously a good thing, but this did delay our exit from Gaza. The other reason, or so our officers explained, was that a tunnel had been found in the area where we were. While combat engineering forces dealt with the tunnel, we stayed to protect them. While we were excited about the ceasefire, we'd been so close to leaving Gaza, and now we found ourselves back in the same exact location.

A few days later, on Friday morning, there was no indication that the ceasefire had been extended. At 5:40 a.m., as I sat listening to music on the radio during my guard shift, the broadcast was suddenly interrupted to announce a rocket had been fired toward the city of Sderot. About an hour later, just before 7:00, another one was reported. The names of the hostages who were to be released that day still hadn't been published by Hamas, and the ceasefire, or so it seemed, was scheduled to end.

IDF tanks got into position in the surrounding area, and the moment the clock struck 7:00 a.m., when the ceasefire was scheduled to end, they opened fire in full force—for what must have been over twenty minutes. It was the most intense barrage I'd heard since entering Gaza. It was the IDF's clear signal that the war was back on.

We packed our bags, knowing that the calm was over and we could be on the move at any moment. About two hours later, we had a briefing about our next mission: to take over Shejaiya, where one of the last fully intact Hamas battalions in northern Gaza was located. This mission would involve the entire 36th Division. We reviewed our objectives as a company and later broke down the details further as a team.

A key part of the plan was that Shejaiya was located near the Israeli border, and our brigade would be attacking from east to west. That meant we would return to Israel for a short break and then launch the operation from the border.

At 8:00 p.m. that night, about thirteen hours after the ceasefire ended, we left our building, boarded trucks, and were successfully brought back into Israel. There was a definite sense of excitement in the air. After nearly four weeks in Gaza, even the smallest things in Israel felt special—like seeing streetlights; Gaza was pitch-black every night.

The ceasefire was over and we were out of Gaza, but not for long. With an understanding that this break was only temporary, we immediately shifted our attention to our next task. The break in Israel was sorely needed, and sleeping without waking up for guard duty was something for which I was truly grateful. After nearly a month in Gaza City, I now understood Gaza, but I was aware that not all areas were the same, and Shejaiya would be uncharted territory.

CHAPTER 11

SHEJAIYA

Shejaiya, December 3–20, 2023

On the news, Gaza is portrayed to be a poor, run-down place often referred to as "the largest open-air prison in the world." Everything I'd seen up to this point contradicted that very idea. Many Gazans were affluent, and the infrastructure I saw wasn't that of tents or shacks, but rather well-built homes, apartment buildings reaching as high as twenty stories in the heart of Gaza City, gyms, restaurants, and a lively scene along the beach. This, obviously, was all before Hamas invaded Israel on October 7, 2023. On the other hand, I also saw tunnels, weapons, and terrorist infrastructure throughout the region. Certainly, a people so poor wouldn't be able to afford things like that, right? Even at a cost to their own people, Hamas prioritized funding terrorist activities.

It was clear, even to an outsider, that Gaza wasn't an ideal place to live. Relatively speaking, Gaza's standard of living appeared to be significantly lower than that of Israel, most of the United States, or anywhere I'd ever consider settling down myself. While many Gazans lived in nice areas, many others did not, and certain areas, although not made up of tents and shacks, were certainly not desirable.

Shejaiya was the first place I saw in Gaza with a significantly lower standard of living. While the Gaza City neighborhood of Zeitoun, where we were several weeks before, was not the nicest, it didn't compare to our time in Shejaiya. For the next two and a half weeks my battalion was stationed there, adjacent to the Israel/Gaza border, and directly across from Nahal Oz, both the kibbutz and army base attacked on October 7. The terrorists who entered that kibbutz and base came from, you guessed it, Shejaiya. And we were about to see it for what it was, a disgusting and dangerous place.

At this point we had been for more than two months straight in the army without a break at home. While two months may not seem long to those accustomed to the US military, where soldiers are deployed for months and months at a time, or stationed, for example, in California with family in New York, serving in the IDF is very different. Israel is a small country, and family and Shabbat are very important, and even in times of war it is both common and expected that soldiers rotate out of battle and get a day at home. While we fully understood the situation we were in and what Israel was facing, the length of time away became noticeable to us and our families.

Several days prior, after the ceasefire came to an end, we left Gaza for a small break. We were brought to Kibbutz Sa'ad, where we stayed for two days and were able to rest. The army gave us mattresses and sleeping bags, and we finally had access to warm portable showers—my first shower in a month! There were tons of food, including a huge barbecue where volunteers came and cooked for us, plus lots of other small comforts and treats.

Most importantly, I got the chance to call home. While we didn't get our personal phones back, people in the area who had phones were happy to lend them to us. I spoke with my brother, my sister, and my parents. When I connected with my sister, she was at Santa-Con, a popular, all-day Santa Claus dress-up celebration in Binghamton, New York, where peppermint and hot cocoa (and possibly alcoholic) drinks flow freely. I recall this clearly because just one year earlier, while in the US during a break in my service, I visited her at school and took part in the festivities.

While these two days in Israel were fun and refreshing, we knew it wouldn't last forever. Maybe it was due to the food or the change of environment, but that Sunday I wasn't feeling well. I had a stomachache, a low-grade fever, and generally felt pretty off. When I saw the doctor, he told me that under normal circumstances he would have sent me home. But because my condition wasn't too severe, and we were heading back to Gaza that night, going home wasn't an option. I wasn't the only one feeling this way—a bunch of others were also sick, and several who were in significantly worse shape than I ended up staying in Israel. A bit before we left for the border that night, I ended up throwing up, which helped. It cleared out my system, and I felt a bit better after that.

Around 11:30 p.m., we loaded onto the Jeeps and headed toward the border, passing by the community of Nahal Oz, right next to Shejaiya, on the Israeli side of the fence. We waited for about three hours in the cold inside the demilitarized zone between the two border fences. Even though it was cold, we were able to get a bit of sleep.

At around 3:30 in the morning, we woke up and began moving into Shejaiya. The walk itself wasn't too long in terms of distance, but it took forever because we kept stopping along the way. At one point, the tanks created a heavy smoke screen. It was so thick we couldn't see more than a couple of meters ahead.

By 6:00 a.m., we reached our first building and waited there for about an hour and a half as the rest of the battalion slowly moved into the area. From there, we advanced another 150 meters to a partially destroyed building that would become our permanent position for the next few days. Despite the damage, it was in decent enough shape.

As I mentioned earlier, Shejaiya was different from where we'd been until then. There weren't tall beachfront buildings, and because this region was still an active Hamas stronghold in which terrorists launched attacks against our troops and fired missiles into Israel, the IDF had already softened the ground for our entry with artillery and air strikes. This entire area, like Gaza City, was also supposed to be cleared of civilians, who were warned multiple times through multiple means that we would be operating there to eliminate Hamas. Many buildings were completely flattened, and even the ones still standing—like the one we were staying in—were badly damaged. Furthermore, the tension in Shejaiya was much higher. Grenades and rockets had already been sent toward our battalion—thankfully not directly at me—but it was clear we were now in a more active zone.

We were stationed on the outskirts of Shejaiya, closest to the Israeli border. Our brigade's most important task was to open and secure the main road for the entire IDF presence in Shejaiya; all logistical movement would come toward our position, and any evacuations would come from our position too.

Our first operation in Shejaiya came two days later, on Wednesday, December 6. Because we'd had that brief break in Israel, and before that the ceasefire, it had been some time since we'd seen any action.

The mission was to take over several buildings as a battalion, about three to four hundred meters north of our current position. Our team was assigned three houses to capture. Before entering the first, we stopped in an open area surrounded by a dirt barrier meant for protection. The area was scattered with tires and logs, and honestly, it looked like a cheap, Hamas version of the obstacle course we went through in the IDF.

The highlight of that moment was that my friend was finally able to fire the Matador rocket he'd been carrying on his back for over a month. The Matador is a hefty rocket weighing just over ten kilograms. The Negev machine gun I carried wasn't light either, but I much preferred it to the Matador. Anyway, he finally took it out, fired it at the target, and hit exactly what he was supposed to, leaving a huge hole in the structure.

After that, we moved on to our first building, taking it over without any issues. Then we moved on to the second, and then the third, capturing each one in turn. We ended up waiting in the last building while the rest of the battalion completed their assignments. While we waited in one apartment, I found a United Nations report from 2014 on housing and urban development in Gaza and the West Bank. I skimmed through it for a bit—it was kind of interesting, at least for passing the time. By 12:30 p.m., we finished the mission and were heading back to our original position.

That night we got a small treat: *sufganiyot*—classic jelly doughnuts. Hanukkah started the next day, and it was quite monumental that we'd spend our first Jewish holiday in Gaza. As an American, I obviously marked my very first Thanksgiving in Gaza as well, but that was irrelevant to everyone around me. I knew this would be a Hanukkah different from all others, and one we'd never forget.

For the next week we marked the Festival of Lights in Gaza. Every night we lit the candles, said the prayers, and received treats. Between *sufganiyot*, gelt, and dreidels, those supporting us in Israel made sure we felt the holiday for what it was. Most interesting of all was how we would light the candles. Normally, the candles on the Chanukiah are not to be blown out because Jewish law says one must wait until the flame goes out on its own. However, in Gaza, to protect ourselves, the rabbinic decision was that we had to blow out the candles after two minutes. Otherwise, during the night, the light would expose us. Getting to light the candles in a safe way summarizes what celebrating Hanukkah in Gaza was like.

Every night we'd do something different. Some nights it was just our team lighting the Chanukiah, and some nights we did so as a company. One night we were accompanied by the commander of our battalion, another night by the second in command. I led the prayers one night, and since the tune we use in America is slightly different from what the Israelis use, that was quite special for me and maybe caused a bit of confusion among my team. Nonetheless, I enjoyed it.

The day after our first operation, we ended up moving positions about three hundred meters up the road, closer to the center of Shejaiya. This house, while we didn't realize it at first, would be one we'd have to get used to—we ended up being stationed there for two weeks, significantly longer than any other house we had positioned ourselves until that point. There were no mattresses, so we slept on our small sleeping pads, the thickness of a yoga mat. This house was dirty, cramped, and gave off weird vibes, but it was home base for the time being.

Over the next several days we didn't go on any operations, but the danger in the region was noticeable. On Saturday, December 9, we were jolted awake at 5:30 a.m. by what was probably the loudest boom we had heard so far. We all shot up and quickly threw on our helmets. Moments later, there was another boom, even louder than the first.

From the sound alone, we could tell these weren't our explosives, and the second boom turned out to be a rocket that, while it didn't hit our building, struck one nearby. It was close enough—and powerful enough—that the shock wave caused our entire building to shake. Bits of debris fell from the ceiling.

While I can't necessarily explain the difference, the sound of IDF firepower has a different ring than that of Hamas. With gunshots alone, there is a difference between our weapons and theirs. Most of the time when I heard noise outside, I'd feel safe knowing that the firepower was coming from the IDF. The ability to detect a slight difference came in handy when something like this occurred. The rocket was clearly that of Hamas.

We waited, fully geared up, for about ten or fifteen minutes, anticipating that more might follow. Instead, the tanks took control of the situation, and when it was relatively quiet, we decided it was okay to go back to sleep.

Over the next week or so, there were two horrible incidents that occurred close to our location. First, a terrorist emerged from a tunnel and attacked a group of Golani soldiers. While responding to the attack, additional soldiers were killed, including several company commanders from Golani and the Magad—the battalion commander—of Golani's 13th Battalion. This battalion, with this commander, was on the front lines on October 7th. They'd been stationed along the Gaza border at the time of the surprise attack, and many in that unit lost their lives that day protecting Israel. Now, just two months later, they suffered another major blow, and this time their battalion commander was one of the victims.

While evacuating wounded soldiers from the initial attack, members of Israel's elite search and rescue team, Unit 669, sought cover in an adjacent building that, unbeknownst to them, had been rigged with explosives. The explosion killed more soldiers. Altogether, it was a devastating chain of events. While we were not directly involved, we could clearly hear the gunfire in the distance and saw the evacuation vehicles rushing past us on their way to Israel. This incident, more than anything else, emphasized just how dangerous and tense the region was.

Several days later, we heard more devastating news that shook the entire country of Israel and Jews everywhere. About half a kilometer from us was the Bislach Brigade, a group of combat soldiers who were training in a commanders course when the war began but were now serving in Gaza.

They were operating in a tense area, in which terrorists had been spotted in the previous days. Tragically, these forces spotted three people emerge from a building and opened fire on what they believed to be Hamas terrorists, but in fact were Israeli hostages who had managed to escape from their captors. This horrible accident emphasized the importance of our actions and our caution. Throughout my time in Gaza, I continually played what-if scenarios with Omer in my head. What if I saw Omer? How would I respond? How would I make sure that my team quickly knew that Omer was innocent, that he was a hostage and not a terrorist? After this tragic incident, those thoughts resurfaced.

During this time, we participated in our longest, possibly most dangerous, and certainly one of the most important missions I'd go on while in Gaza. The goal was to take over the main Hamas base in Shejaiya, which was no small task. This wasn't just a mission for our battalion—it was a brigade-wide operation.

Before getting into the details, a few points are worth mentioning. Hamas terrorists are smart enough not to remain on their own bases—they know we'll eventually come for them. Instead, they mostly hide in tunnels underground or in civilian homes. Still, the IDF has to take over their bases, and there are always critical things to find. And since this was a brigade-level mission, everything took longer—there were a lot of moving parts to coordinate.

We left around 9:00 in the morning and walked about four hundred meters east. Before turning north for another six hundred meters, we waited at a junction for about two hours. We were delayed because we had to wait for another battalion in the brigade to complete their movement. Once they finished, we continued our advance and waited a bit more. It wasn't until around 1:00 p.m. that we started moving directly toward our destination.

Most teams, including ours, were tasked with taking over buildings surrounding the Hamas base to help secure the entire area. Once that was complete, Yahalom would enter the base itself. Hamas knows we'll eventually enter, so they often plant explosives in and around the base, making these operations significantly more dangerous.

Accompanying our team were two Yahalom soldiers—true experts at identifying explosives—and a squad from Oketz, the dog unit. These specially trained dogs were equipped with a camera and were sent into buildings before soldiers would enter to help ensure they were safe. These dogs ended up saving our lives.

As we approached our destination, our commander pointed out the two buildings we needed to take over, one on the left and one on the right. After tanks shelled both buildings, as is standard before entry, we approached the house on the left. I noticed a mark on the exterior wall and flagged it to my commander. Before entering Gaza, we were briefed about how Hamas would booby-trap buildings with explosives and then leave secretive marks to indicate to other Hamas members that a booby trap had been set and not to enter.

Since we weren't certain if there was an explosive set, we approached carefully and sent the Oketz dog in first. In the footage taken by the camera attached to the dog, something seemed suspicious to one of the

Yahalom soldiers. He slowly peeked inside for a closer look, and that is when he spotted a massive explosive. According to him, this type of explosive, if triggered, could have collapsed the entire building and killed everyone inside. Thanks to the Oketz dog and the expertise of the Yahalom soldier, our lives were saved. This ended up being one of the most, if not the most, dangerous moments of my life.

Just to further set the scene, as I said, since I had the Negev gun, I was always stationed in the front of our team when we advanced, right next to my commander. I was almost always the first soldier on my team to enter any building, something I didn't tell my mother until I completed my service. If the explosive hadn't been spotted, we would have entered the building, and I would have been the first hit. Many IDF soldiers lost their lives in Gaza in situations exactly like this. I was fortunate, as was my team, that the dog detected the explosive, and that we had experts from Yahalom with us. Our lives were saved, and it was the professionalism of the IDF we had to thank for it.

Since that first building was too dangerous, we moved on to the second, right next door, and took it over. After the entire area surrounding the base was secure, Yahalom entered the base to perform their operations.

The next day we learned what they'd found. In addition to military gear and weapons, which are commonly found throughout Gaza, Yahalom uncovered some critical intelligence. Among the finds were Hamas's plans to attack IDF soldiers in Shejaiya. More significantly, detailed maps of the entire underground tunnel system in Shejaiya were found. This was huge. Hamas primarily operates through its underground tunnel network, and having a full map of it was a major breakthrough. With this information, the IDF could more effectively destroy the tunnels, making it far more difficult for the Hamas battalion in Shejaiya to function. Despite the difficulties we faced in this war, findings like these demonstrated exactly why it was so important that we were in Gaza: to bring about the destruction of Hamas and, more importantly, the return of all the hostages.

As the days went on in Gaza, one thing became clear: We needed a break. The issue, however, was that our mission in Shejaiya kept getting extended. Originally, we were told we'd only be there for two to five days, a respectable time. But every time we were given a date we were leaving, it was postponed. This happened several times. In the end we were in Shejaiya for nineteen days. We finally left on Wednesday, December 20.

On that morning, we woke up to fantastic news: We thought we would be delayed again, but the word going around was that we were really leaving Gaza. We didn't believe it at first—there were always delays and disappointments—but this time the rumor felt more real than other times, and that gave us hope.

Our commander told us to have our bags packed by 5:30 that afternoon and to make sure we didn't leave anything behind. We were told we'd be leaving at around 8:00 p.m., and we sat around and waited. And waited. I even managed to sleep a bit. As always, there was a delay, and we thought we might not end up leaving after all. But then, at 10:45 p.m., we were given the green light. Hurling our bags onto our backs, we walked outside. I couldn't believe it; we were actually leaving Gaza.

We walked over two kilometers past the border and all the way to Kibbutz Nahal Oz. It was a tougher walk than I expected, but none of that mattered—we were out of Shejaiya and back in Israel.

We loaded onto buses and made our way to a base in Ashkelon, where we'd spend the night and the next day. Out of all the good news we received, the best by far was this: Not only were we out of Gaza, but we were going to get some time at home, away from the army. After eighty-two straight days in the IDF, everyone was beyond excited. Though it looked like we would return to Gaza the following week, for now, we were back in civilization.

CHAPTER 12

CENTRAL GAZA

*Central Gaza, December 27, 2023
–January 11, 2024*

On January 4, 2022, my day of enlistment to the IDF, my first stop—the first stop for *all* soldiers drafting into the IDF—was the Bakum at Tel Hashomer, the IDF's enlistment center in Ramat Gan. Like the first day of school, I had jitters in my stomach as I underwent medical testing, received vaccinations, and tried on my uniform for the first time in what felt like a combination of a large men's locker room and clothing store dressing room.

Most importantly, that day I received my *choger*. The *choger*, or military ID card, is something that never leaves your sight until your final day in the army. Typically, this ID card can be found in the front pocket of your uniform, and in training especially, it's vital that a commander never finds this missing.

The *choger* contains some pretty important information: name, military ID number, enlistment date, and most important of all, release date. When I received my *choger*, I checked that my release date was listed as January 3, 2024. Because I was already twenty-one years old when I made *aliyah* and became an Israeli citizen, I was only required to serve two years in the IDF, and I was glad to see that my *choger* reflected just that. For context, the other men I served with, eighteen- or nineteen-year-olds, Israeli born and raised, were required to serve two years eight months, so on the date I was scheduled to complete my service, they still had plenty of time left.

Fast forward two years, and my service, clearly, took an unexpected turn. Instead of preparing for life after the army, I had just finished over a month and a half operating in the Gaza Strip. Now, on December 25, 2023, after several days away from Gaza, my battalion was planning to reenter.

Before returning to my unit, I was given a choice by my commanders. Since my required service was supposed to end on January 3, 2024, and we were expected to stay in Gaza beyond that date, I was given the option not to reenter Gaza but serve out my last days in the IDF in Israel. This was not an easy decision, and I was offered advice by many. But, with the war still at its peak, and recalling the promise I made to myself earlier not to leave Gaza without Omer, I decided I would continue on with my team.

Logistically, this meant that until January 3, 2024, I would serve as an active-duty soldier and, the next day, on January 4, I would automatically convert to a reserve soldier. Reserve soldiers receive higher pay and are given more rights, but that was quite frankly the last thing on my mind. The important thing was that I was going back to Gaza with my team.

The previous week had been one of great excitement as well as rest.

Finally, after eighty-two days straight in the army, we were given a break at home. Just to give you some context, the longest I spent in the army without a break prior to that was nineteen days, which meant I was on base for three weeks and then got that third weekend off. Usually, I'd never spend more than two weeks straight on base, and oftentimes even less than a week, depending on when and what we were up to.

So, after eighty-two days without a break from the army, and after more than a month and a half inside Gaza, we finally returned to Israel from Shejaiya on Wednesday night, December 20, 2023. We were brought to the Kfar Nofesh base located on the beach in Ashkelon, which is designed specifically for soldiers to rest and relax.

The next day, while still at the Kfar Nofesh base in Ashkelon, we attended some meetings to prepare us for our next round in Gaza but also had the opportunity to enjoy everything the base had to offer, including massages, haircuts, great food—everything you'd expect at an all-inclusive resort, just on an army base. Plus, we were reunited with some of our personal items, like our cell phones, which we last had on November 3.

That night, we were released to go home for Shabbat with instructions to return on Sunday morning. The problem for me (and some others) was, *Where's home?* Before October 7th, my home was Kibbutz Erez, right along the Gaza border, but the kibbutz was evacuated that day and its residents, including my host family, were sent to Mitzpe Ramon, a small city in the middle of the Negev desert. So, I decided to spend my little break with them.

The weekend was relaxing, low-key, exactly what I needed. What defined my weekend in Mitzpe Ramon was just how kind my host family was to me. They provided me with everything I needed, took me out for some delicious meals, and even decorated my hotel room with cards made by several kids in the community. During this time, I spoke often with my family back in New York and learned that they planned to visit Israel the following week with the hope of seeing me if I was not in Gaza.

On Sunday morning, on the drive back to my base, my host father had to stop in Kibbutz Erez for a bit, and I went with him. Seeing the kibbutz after October 7th was very emotional, with all the decorations from the holiday of Sukkot that remained up, almost three months after it had ended.

The transition from home to base is always difficult, but this time was more difficult than most. We weren't just returning to base; we were returning to Gaza. All of Sunday and Monday was spent preparing our gear and being briefed on our mission, and heading to sleep Monday evening, we were told we'd be waking up at around 3:30 a.m. on Tuesday morning to leave base by 4:00.

That morning, we were taken by bus to a field near Ofakim, where we transferred to Jeeps that would take us to the Gaza border. By midmorning, we arrived at a spot fewer than one hundred meters from the border, waiting to enter. We expected a short wait—maybe thirty minutes—but, as usual, time stretched on. Eventually, we were told our entry to Gaza was postponed until the next morning.

Instead of returning to base, we'd spend the night outside, near the border. We were given food, made a bonfire, and settled in for the night. Sitting around that fire just a few hundred meters from Gaza felt like the calm before the storm. I felt as if I was at camp sitting with friends, ready to burst out into campfire songs. The only difference was that instead of camp, we were several hundred meters from Gaza, and instead of heading to our bunks afterward, we were about to head into a battle zone. That night I went to sleep under the open sky, mentally preparing for what the next morning would bring.

As scheduled, on Wednesday, December 27, we were up by 3:00 a.m., made our way toward Gaza, and crossed the border by 4:00. We began our trek toward the El Bureij refugee camp—the place we were assigned to for the next few weeks.

The walk itself was difficult. Rather than a direct path, it was full of zigzags and frequent breaks. As we approached our destination, the building we were tasked with clearing out, my commander told me to open fire toward it. But as I began shooting, my gun jammed. The middle part, called the *michlol*, was stuck—a critical part of the weapon. I needed a hard surface to strike the gun against to loosen it, but we were on sand, so it was hard to find the leverage I needed.

Because my weapon wasn't functioning, the other soldier on my team with a Negev took my place up front, and I retreated to the back of the group. Once we secured the building, I was able to successfully unjam my gun.

After clearing the first building, we proceeded to take over another house that was relatively small, only one story. This house became our first home base in Central Gaza, and now we were ready for any operation.

A few days later, December 29, ended up being an exciting and successful day in Gaza as we were tasked with advancing and taking over two buildings. As we made our way to the first, we noticed markings that could indicate the presence of Hamas explosives. We approached with extreme caution, with the Oketz unit's dogs entering each house first to scan for bombs.

In the first house, the dogs discovered something odd—a live dog (not one of the Oketz dogs) just lying there. This raised serious suspicion. It could mean someone had recently been there. Another possibility was that Hamas intentionally placed a dog inside to distract our dog, preventing it from properly completing its search. Either way, this was the only time I witnessed something like this throughout my time in Gaza.

Then, before entering the first building, I had the opportunity to throw in a grenade—my first time doing so. The point was to destroy any potential explosives inside and, if necessary, neutralize any terrorist present. There were none, as expected, but using a grenade was a standard safety procedure. Once we secured the building, we discovered several grenades and military vests, but nothing more significant.

In the second building, we found four large explosives, but, more significantly, the Yahalom unit, with other soldiers from my team, uncovered a tunnel entrance hidden among the trees outside. At the entrance to the tunnel, they found a rocket launcher and other equipment. Yahalom blew up the site, destroying the tunnel and any chance of Hamas using that area for operations again anytime soon.

New Year's Eve means gathering around the television with my family, waiting for the iconic moment the ten-second countdown begins and the ball in Times Square drops as thousands of crazy people stand outside in frigid temperatures all day specifically for this moment. New Year's Eve 2024 would obviously be very different for me as I spent it in the Gaza Strip.

I was scheduled for guard duty that night from midnight to 1:00 a.m., when the New Year began. I asked a friend who was on shift before me to wake me up several minutes early so I could listen to the radio at midnight, a way for me to connect to the outside world. I wanted to hear the radio hosts wish everyone a Happy New Year.

With the radio by my side, my weapon pointed outdoors, and my eyes looking into the distance, I suddenly saw rockets launched several hundred meters south just as it turned midnight. Seconds later, as the radio hosts were wishing everyone in Israel a Happy New Year, they were interrupted by the red alert—*tzevah adom* warnings of incoming rockets toward Tel Aviv and the surrounding area. For the first time, I saw rockets being launched from Gaza toward Israel and felt that I could have alerted the public. Just as New Yorkers celebrated with the Times Square ball and others celebrated with fireworks, Hamas marked the stroke of midnight with rockets fired toward Israel.

While the New Year started with a red alert, that day would end up being one of the most important and meaningful days yet. Several hours after my guard shift, our team was awakened at 4:30 a.m., earlier than usual. Apparently—and we had only learned of this that morning—there was some intelligence that either living or dead hostages might be in the area, and this was to be our focus for the second half of the day. By 5:15 a.m., we were already out the door.

Advancing, we took over our first building. Not too long after that, I was pulled with several other members of my team to clear a building right next door. I wasn't sure if the IDF or anyone in my unit had intelligence on what we were about to discover, but it would be a major find.

Soon I entered the ground level of a three-story building, where the first floor was a warehouse and the second two floors were residential apartments, and immediately noticed something special. Right in front of us were huge qassam rockets and rocket launchers. Qassams are large rockets used to shoot long distances; in the case of Hamas, toward Tel Aviv, Jerusalem, and the surrounding areas. This was a huge moment for my battalion.

This marked a great achievement for me. This find wasn't just for my battalion, it was for me, for my squad. I was a part of finding this, and the next day when the radio station reported about it, and as I sat listening to the news in Gaza, a huge sense of pride came over me as I understood my part in the mission. These rockets would be brought back to Israel for research and, obviously, so that Hamas wouldn't have them.

After this, we made our way to a kindergarten, which was where intelligence believed there might be either dead or living hostages. I don't know if the intelligence was wrong, or if Hamas had hostages there at one point and cleaned up their mess, but we found nothing, which was very disappointing.

Inside the kindergarten, it was weird to see the date on the whiteboard—October 5, 2023, the Thursday before the attack, the last school day in Gaza. This reminded me of all the Sukkahs still standing in kibbutzim in the Gaza Envelope months after the war began. The region, ever since that dark Saturday, has been frozen in time on both sides of the border.

The next few days were relatively uneventful, and I sat with my team in a nice house in El Bureij. Our entire operational responsibility was to guard the main logistics road into the area. Every few hours I'd have guard duty and look over the road, scanning the area for anything suspicious.

Despite the calm, there were some significant milestones. As I explained before, January 3, 2024, was my last official day in the army, and I officially became a reserve soldier on January 4. While we marked this moment with a little cheer, I insisted that the main celebration would come when I officially finished my time in Gaza, and when Omer and every hostage returned home. Since my friends in the army still had many months left in their service, this moment was only significant for me.

Two days later, I celebrated my twenty-fourth birthday. There was significance in celebrating while in Gaza, and it didn't go without a birthday cake. My parents and siblings were in Israel, hoping to see me, and decided to bake cakes to be brought into Gaza. This, as I learned later, was a challenge. They needed to figure out a way to make a cake that would last without refrigeration, and that wouldn't melt or lose its form. They got in touch with the logistics team that brought us supplies, dropped them off at my base, and when our next delivery of supplies arrived, I was shocked to find four cakes, one with "Happy Birthday Ira" written in sprinkles. The cakes were squished and beat up during their journey into Gaza, but they were delicious and much appreciated.

Idan Amedi is one of Israel's most popular artists, and there is a special reason why. At the age of eighteen, he enlisted in the IDF, along with most of his Israeli peers and began his service in the combat engineering brigade. Following his service, Idan went onto the show *Kochav Nolad—A Star Is Born* (Israel's version of *American Idol*)—where he performed his song "Ke'ev shel Lochamim," "Pain of a Warrior," which became an instant hit. His music career progressed, his fame increased, and he was soon cast as Sagi Tzur on the Netflix hit show *Fauda*. He was now a star, though he never viewed himself as such.

On October 7, Amedi grabbed his gun. He told the country that he was prepared to go over a year without performing and would join his brothers and sisters by joining the reserves and protecting Israel. Imagine that: a pop star and world-known actor putting everything aside to protect his country.

On January 8, 2024, Amedi was serving with his combat engineering unit in Central Gaza not far from where I was located with my unit.

There was a terrible incident in which many IDF soldiers were killed and many more injured. We were supposed to advance to a new position the following day, but due to this incident, our advance was postponed. The next day we found out that not only were many soldiers killed or injured, but one of the injured was Idan Amedi. He was airlifted to a hospital, underwent several surgeries, and although grateful he was alive, his fans and supporters feared he would never be able to perform onstage again.

On January 6, 2025, two days short of a year after being injured, Amedi released a new album, *Superman*, that took the nation by storm. He began performing again, bringing life and hope to a people still healing from war, and with hostages still in Gaza. He represents your average Israeli grabbing his gun and doing his part to protect his country when the time called. He symbolizes a successful recovery from a dark place and showed the nation that despite the war and hardships, we could once again stand up and return to our passions. His performances are often marked by pictures of him holding flags of fallen soldiers, dedicating his music to those who sacrificed their lives for our country.

On May 25, 2025, more than a year after I returned to New York from the war, I learned Idan Amedi was coming to Long Island for a special evening of conversation and song. This was an opportunity I couldn't pass up. I went to hear him perform and afterward took a picture with him wearing my #BringOmerHome shirt and holding up a picture of my friend Yair Avitan, killed while fighting in Gaza. This moment, of meeting my favorite Israeli artist, made me tremendously happy. He is a true hero of Israel, with whom I feel I have a special connection because we both served in the same area at the same time. One Israeli star, one simple Jewish boy from Long Island.

On Wednesday, January 10, my team advanced to a new location on a three-kilometer trek that stretched through a beautiful area of Gaza. While Gaza City had nicer buildings and was right along the beach, the nature here, especially the abundance of trees, was a rare sight for us.

Advancing in the open fields, we looked to our right to see the major neighborhoods of Central Gaza along the coast, mainly intact. Salah Al Deen is a major road that cuts north to south through the middle of Gaza, and while the IDF ground forces were operating to the east of that road in Central Gaza, west of that road was mainly untouched, and it was rare to see a huge area of standing buildings. The belief was that many of the hostages were being held there, and it remained, throughout the war, an area with little to no military activity.

Along this walk, a team in front of us found an entrance to a tunnel, and it was the responsibility of my team to protect the entrance until members of the Combat Engineering corps arrived to deal with it further. Tunnel entrances come in different shapes and sizes. Some tunnel entrances are inside buildings, like the one we found in the Gaza City mosque, but this was just a hole in the ground in the great outdoors, looking like a large anthill.

Eventually, we made it to our destination, were assigned a house, and set up the place to make it more comfortable. This house was crowded, as several teams from our battalion were assigned there. My commanders learned my family had traveled to Israel specifically to see me, and because we were scheduled to leave Gaza in a few days anyway, I received permission to leave Gaza early to see my family.

When the next day came, excitement boiled up inside me. For the first time since starting our operations in Gaza, I'd have the chance to see my family. However, as the day went on and the waiting continued, frustration settled in. I was supposed to leave in the morning, but that was postponed. My new time was noon, then once again postponed to 4:00 p.m. I made my way outside, loaded onto a vehicle, and then was told to get off because we couldn't leave until evening. Frustrated beyond belief, I lost hope that I'd get to see my family that day.

By evening, I waited by the walkie-talkie until I finally got word that it was time to leave. I took my gun loaded onto the vehicle, and we soon were on our way to Israel. After my third trip inside the Gaza Strip, I was finally back on the other side of the border.

I was with my family, which was exciting, but the next steps for my battalion were unclear, and I was no longer in active service, so I didn't know what my own next steps would be. At least I would enjoy being with my family while I could.

CHAPTER 13

KHAN YUNIS

Khan Yunis, January 18–February 28, 2024

It was Thursday, January 11, when I left Gaza, and I was able to spend Shabbat with my parents, brother, and sister. It was calming to spend the day of rest truly resting from the war. We even had relatives over for Shabbat dinner that Friday night. I left in the middle to fall asleep; that's how tired I was.

On Saturday night, I went with my family to Hostage Square, the name given to the plaza in front of the Tel Aviv Art Museum where each Saturday night since the start of the war people would gather to call for the return of the hostages. It became a makeshift memorial with signs and posters to honor and remember those held in Gaza. This Saturday night marked one hundred days since October 7th, which was an unimaginable milestone to reach, though we didn't know at the time that it would continue much longer.

Having just left the war zone of Gaza, I found the crowds, bright lights, and tall buildings of Tel Aviv overwhelming. However, watching Israelis fight for the hostages gave me hope and meaning as I saw a different battle take place away from the actual battlefield. Although it was not with guns and in front of terrorists, advocating for the hostages was just as important. For the first time since the start of the war, I also saw Orna and Ronen Neutra, Omer's parents, still fighting for their son's release. At this rally they spoke to a crowd of thousands.

The next day my family was on their way back to the United States, and I went back to the base. I learned that my friends were leaving Gaza that next morning for a short break, but that in several days we'd be reentering Gaza again, and almost certainly going to Khan Yunis, in the southern part of the strip. Hearing the news, I knew my time in the army was far from over. Now that I'd finished my active service, I did, after all, have a choice of whether or not to continue. But as Omer was still a hostage and my friends in the army were still entering Gaza, I knew I wasn't finished.

I joined my battalion at Ir HaBahadim, a large, campus-like base in the Negev desert where we prepared for our reentry to Gaza. This base is so big that it's literally called a city—*ir*, in Hebrew. Our next round in Gaza was going to feel different. For the first time we were heading to an area full of Gazans. While we wouldn't operate in any areas where civilians resided, Khan Yunis, as compared to other areas we'd been, still had civilians present. The IDF released very clear maps and directions for the residents of Gaza so they would know where it was safe to be and where it was not in Khan Yunis. In some areas of the city, literally one side of the road was safe and the other side wasn't, and we only operated where civilians had been told to leave.

I was looking forward to this time in Gaza because of my new GoPro. After almost three months in Gaza, many of my friends had brought in body cameras to document some of what we experienced. I decided to get a GoPro for that exact purpose, and I spent time adjusting the camera comfortably on my vest so I could take a good video while not interfering with my ability to operate.

Eventually, after the regular last-minute preparations and checks of our equipment, including turning in our phones once again, we were on our way to the border, where we'd wait to be taken into Gaza. After a long wait, we finally got onto the vehicles and made the thirty-minute drive into Khan Yunis.

The next few days were relatively calm. We stayed in the same area with no real operation or task at hand, except to protect the area we were in. We then advanced several days later.

One of the things that stood out now, as compared to other times in Gaza, was just how far we were from Israel. As compared to other areas of Gaza, the south is wider, so much of Khan Yunis is farther from Israel than more northern areas of the strip. This became most noticeable when we tried making phone calls to Israel and even when listening to the radio.

The mood shifted quickly when we heard about two deadly incidents that happened nearby. In the first, several officers from the 202nd Battalion of the paratroopers were killed in our vicinity. It hit close to home because these were fellow paratroopers, but the second incident was far worse. Twenty-one combat engineering soldiers were killed when a missile struck the building they were in while placing explosives. The missile triggered the charges, causing a massive explosion and devastating losses. I wasn't exactly sure of all the details at the time, but I learned later just how devastating it was, the deadliest incident since October 7th.

With this news, it was easy to feel how different—and how much more dangerous—Khan Yunis was. Just the day before, a terrorist was killed right next to the building we were in. Up until then, Shejaiya had felt like the most dangerous area we'd operated in, but Khan Yunis surpassed it. There was a tension in the air that was hard to describe, and it felt as if people—whether Hamas terrorists or civilians, I didn't know—were still very much around.

There was also a lot of intelligence pointing to hostage activity in this area, along with evidence of terrorist activity. About half a kilometer west of our location, there reportedly were half a million Gazans. The rest were believed to be concentrated in Rafah and Central Gaza. Knowing how populated the area still was made things more complicated for us operationally.

Another major difference was the sheer concentration of IDF forces. In past missions, we were always aware that the IDF was operating in other parts of Gaza simultaneously. This time, we were the main IDF operation. Most of the IDF had pulled out of other areas of the strip, focusing whatever forces remained alongside us. We were no longer just part of the operation anymore—we were the operation.

On Thursday, January 25, we left our present location and advanced southwest for our first offensive since entering Khan Yunis. Although we had been in the city for a week, our responsibilities were limited and mundane. Now, things were about to get busy.

Advancing deeper into the area, we took over and cleared our designated building. After finishing the attack, we fired southward in the direction of the enemy—the direction where the IDF had yet to enter—and allowed other teams in our battalion to advance and take over their designated buildings. The plan was to advance farther south on Friday.

A few members of my team—excluding me—headed to the first building to blow a hole in the exterior wall for entry. We never, and I mean never, entered a building through the front door due to the danger of Hamas explosives. A D9 truck—a large military bulldozer— would usually create an opening in an exterior wall for us to safely enter, but due to the location of this building, and because the road was more like an alley, the D9 truck couldn't fit. Therefore, several friends on my team, using explosives we carried, blew a hole in the wall themselves. The process was impressive to watch.

After about twenty minutes, they came back—not just with a hole in the wall, but also with a Gazan man who had seen them and surrendered immediately. They brought him back to our position, and some of the senior officers in our battalion arrived to handle the situation. They spoke with him in Arabic and learned that he had two sons actively serving in Hamas, as well as two daughters married to Hamas terrorists.

The man looked to be in his sixties or seventies, and although he was not supposed to be in the area, he was not harmed because he surrendered and ended up providing valuable intelligence. I wasn't sure where they took him afterward, but I assumed he was brought back to Israel for further questioning. What made the whole situation surreal was that, after three months in Gaza, aside from the ceasefire, this was the first time I had seen a Gazan alive—emphasis on alive. Up until then, I hadn't seen a single Gazan face-to-face.

Before we headed out on our mission the following morning, we were told that the day before a team in our battalion had found two dog tags belonging to hostages—one apparently from a tank unit. The officer who informed us didn't remember the names of the hostages, but he said he would check. Since one of them was from the tanks, my thoughts immediately went to Omer. I tried not to dwell on it too much, but I was anxious to find out whose dog tags they had found. A few days later, I was disappointed to learn that it wasn't him.

Before we even left on the mission, something unexpected and unwelcome happened. We were sitting in the apartment when we suddenly heard a boom from upstairs. It wasn't anything massive, so we assumed something had just fallen—especially because some of our team members were up there. A minute later, one of them came down and casually said that a rocket had just hit our building. He said it so calmly. Our commander went up to check and confirmed it—a piece of the rocket was there. It wasn't a large rocket and based on where we were positioned in the building, we wouldn't have been hit anyway. We had placed ourselves on the opposite side from where the threat would come, exactly for situations like this. But it was a wild way to start the day.

From there, we went out on our mission. This one was different—we ended up taking over four buildings, all right next to one another and almost physically connected. This area of Khan Yunis, known as the refugee camp, was so dense that many of the buildings were touching. Only the last building we took over was slightly set apart from the rest. These buildings had strange layouts and odd structural quirks that made the mission more complicated than usual, but nothing we couldn't handle.

The second building really stood out. It was unusually fancy, with a nice two-story apartment, a beautiful chandelier (a rare sight here), and, overall, it looked very different from the rest. Even more surprising was the ground floor: It had a full gym, packed with brand-new machines, weights, and everything you'd expect to see in a commercial fitness center. Finding something like that in Gaza, especially during a war, felt bizarre.

Just fifty meters from where we were—literally across the street—was a hospital. Gazans were freely walking around the compound. The hospital was considered a humanitarian zone, and therefore off-limits for IDF attacks. Southern Gaza, specifically Khan Yunis, was divided by the IDF into designated zones: some where we operated and others where civilians were allowed to stay safely. This was the first time I saw so many Gazans in one place, walking around as if we weren't conducting operations just across the street.

Throughout the mission, our battalion identified several armed terrorists right outside the hospital perimeter. At one point, some soldiers spotted a terrorist running into the hospital compound, presumably thinking he would be safe there. From our perspective, these terrorists were using civilians as human shields, exploiting humanitarian zones for protection.

My team engaged and took down several armed individuals inside the compound that day. The terrorists, by running with weapons into a humanitarian zone, had turned it into a combat zone. It was a difficult and ugly situation—both tactically and morally. But we knew that if Hamas could freely exploit these zones, it would only encourage more of the same. These areas were supposed to protect civilians, not shelter armed combatants.

What I witnessed that day was exactly what we had heard about on the news. However, this time, I saw it up close and personal. We knew that Hamas used civilian areas to protect their military operations, and this was the clearest example of that. To witness this unfold was surreal, but it validated everything I knew about Hamas. That day ended up being one of the craziest of all, and we weren't done.

The next morning, we woke up at 5:00 a.m. because we were scheduled to advance and attack a new location. But, as always, there was a delay—we didn't end up leaving until 7:00. We then began the trek and made our way into a house that had already been taken over by another team in our battalion, where we waited for our turn to push forward. Just like the day before, when we took over four buildings lined up one after the next, we did the same thing again. It really highlighted just how cramped Khan Yunis is—buildings stacked on top of one another. The area we were operating in was considered the main refugee camp of Khan Yunis, so it made sense that everything felt so packed together.

That same day, the commander of our battalion, the Magad, gave each of his several hundred soldiers a picture of a hostage to fit in our vest pockets right above our hearts. The idea was to always keep the hostages front and center. We were here for them, and hopefully our efforts would not only bring about the destruction of Hamas, but the return of every last hostage. I was given a picture of Bar Kuperstein, a young man about my age who was working as a guard and paramedic at the Nova Music Festival and was taken hostage into Gaza. He was taken alive, and his picture stayed in my vest until my last days fighting in Gaza. After my service, that picture made its way into my wallet. I am thrilled to report that Bar was returned, alive, to Israel on October 13, 2025, after more than two years in Hamas captivity.

The next several days we, the 35th Paratrooper Brigade, continued advancing southward and taking over buildings, while the 7th Armored Brigade was advancing northward. They were currently only a few hundred meters south of us, and the area in between was likely where the enemy was still hiding within the city. With every move, we were pushing deeper into Khan Yunis, tightening the gap and eliminating the enemy, their weapons, and their infrastructure. It was a busy and productive week with little sleep.

As I mentioned, one of the interesting yet also complex things about my time in Khan Yunis was our proximity to and interaction with Gazan civilians, which is something we didn't experience elsewhere in Gaza. One day the IDF opened a humanitarian corridor allowing Gazan civilians in Khan Yunis another opportunity to move west to safe humanitarian zones. During this time my team was stationed with the snipers in our unit. They were equipped with very strong binoculars and scopes on their guns, and I had the opportunity to look through them to see clearly what I couldn't with my own eyes. I saw floods of people moving along the path—whole groups evacuating. It was surreal to see how many civilians were still in the area after so many announcements from the IDF urging them to leave. Watching that many people evacuate all at once was intense—both from a humanitarian and an operational perspective. This was certainly one of the more interesting things I witnessed in Gaza.

The following day, we conducted what was at this point an ordinary advance, clearing and searching buildings for terrorists. But what stood out was the location of our operation—it was right next to a designated humanitarian zone, where we weren't allowed to engage. In one of the buildings we secured, we posted guards in several directions, and one of those was facing the humanitarian area. From our position, we could clearly see many Gazans walking around freely. It felt strange to be so close to people with whom we were technically at war—less than one hundred meters away—and yet we were just watching, not reacting.

I couldn't help but think: *What if one of them is a bad guy?* It felt odd, knowing we could see them but weren't doing anything—until or unless they crossed the line. The rules were clear: They were allowed to be in that area, and if they crossed into ours, we had permission to respond. Additionally, if we saw someone in the humanitarian zone carrying a weapon, we were authorized to shoot, as we would not allow Hamas to turn these humanitarian zones into combat zones.

In another situation, our unit searched a large, abandoned school complex after all civilians were once again told to evacuate. Hamas very often uses schools to launch rockets and hide weapons, so it was necessary to search this area carefully. During the operation, our company found one person still inside. He turned out to be the school janitor and appeared to have mental health issues, but he was still questioned briefly to try to gather any information he might have before he was released. He was taken from the combat zone, given Bamba (a popular Israeli snack) and other snacks, and brought to a safer area.

There was nothing otherwise noteworthy about this time other than the house that would become our home for a few days. It was interesting for one reason and one reason only: the chickens. On the floor above us was a whole chicken flock, and instead of staying in a confined coop, the chickens were roaming around freely. Our task was to try to keep the chickens out! The chickens made it to our living quarters a handful of times and shooing them away became comedic relief in and of itself.

As the IDF continued its work in Khan Yunis, shrinking the areas in which Hamas could operate and evacuating civilians to safe humanitarian zones, it was decided that each company in my battalion would get a short one- or two-day break from being in Gaza. Our break would come on Sunday, February 11, and as you can imagine, this gave us something to really look forward to.

Before we knew it, we were on trucks back to Israel, and after a quick transfer to buses near Kibbutz Magen, we made our way to the Tzanhanim training base, arriving around 9:30 p.m. The rest of the night was relaxing and enjoyable, and I was excited to be out of Gaza.

That night, however, was something special, especially for me—it was the Super Bowl! It felt very odd because if I were not in the army in the middle of a war, I would have been very tuned into the NFL playoffs and looking forward to the game. But because I was completely exhausted, I only managed to watch about a quarter of the game. However, the greatest play that night did not occur in the Super Bowl;

instead, it happened thousands of miles away in Rafah. That night, two hostages, Fernando Marman and Luis Har, were rescued alive by IDF special forces. This was the ultimate touchdown and not only were we happy to have a break from Gaza, but we were also ecstatic that two hostages were finally home.

Now, knowing that we'd be back inside the Gaza Strip in just a few days, the goal during this small break was to take it easy, to rest and recuperate as much as we could. Until Wednesday, that was exactly what I did.

I also decided to use this time to decide whether this was the right time to finish my service or if it made more sense to continue with my team. As I mentioned earlier, because I was now a reserve soldier, the decision was mine. However, I realized I had to come back once we left Gaza a day earlier. After this strange half-break, we returned to the exact same place in Gaza we left. And I wanted to stay with my team for as long as we were still on the mission in Khan Yunis.

So, on Wednesday, February 14, it was back to business. We headed straight to the Gaza Envelope, and after a few hours of organizing our gear, we were on our way back to the Strip, returning to the same area and sleeping in a building right next to where we were before the break.

Throughout the next few days, we performed the same type of operations over and over again. There were specific buildings in the area that had to be destroyed, and one of the main ways we did that was by placing landmines in the buildings and blowing them up. This task was usually done by combat engineering teams, but there were very few of their soldiers with us, so we were given the task instead.

About a week and a half later, I had one of my busiest days in Gaza. The goal for the day was to take over a neighborhood in the northern part of Khan Yunis that hadn't yet been captured by the IDF. This neighborhood was over two kilometers away from our current position, which is considered a relatively far distance—especially in the heart of Khan Yunis. Just think about that: IDF forces walk two full kilometers into the heart of a major Gaza city. That's certainly not something that could have happened just a few months prior.

That morning, we woke up around 5:00 a.m., though I was up an hour earlier for guard duty. We gathered all of our gear, double-checked that we weren't leaving anything behind, and by 6:00 a.m. we were out the door.

We ended up taking over seven or eight houses that day, one after the other. Each one seemed smaller, filthier, and more run-down than the last—clearly not the nicest part of Khan Yunis.

That day, another company in our battalion encountered a group of around thirty or forty Gazans, who surrendered. These were full families—men, women, and children. The soldiers handled the situation by separating the men from the women and children, searching the men, and running their identities through the system. In the end, four men were taken for further questioning, and the rest—including all the women and children—were let go. They were given food and water, pointed in a safe direction, and sent on their way.

That moment stuck with me. If the roles had been reversed, I know the outcome would not have been the same. Let's be honest—Hamas would have taken hostages. But this is what sets us apart. We let them go, and while it was a strange thing to watch unfold, I understand that this was the IDF's protocol, and certainly something I agree with. If they are not there to harm us, there is no reason to hold them or harm them.

By the end of the day, I was completely exhausted. I also started feeling a lot more pain in my lower back and stomach, something that had been building for a while now, but had become worse with all the weight I carried and the intense activity. After a long hour of guard duty, I finally got into bed and passed out.

We continued with similar missions for several days until February 28, which ended up being our final day in Gaza. As usual, for hours we sat around and waited for the green light to pack up our bags and leave. In the late afternoon, we were suddenly told to get ready quickly—our departure had been moved up. Not only were we going to be the first team from our battalion to leave, but we were the first team in the entire Paratrooper Brigade to head out. We rushed to prepare our bags and made our way outside to begin the walk to the pickup location. Unlike the usual frustrating walks with our heavy bags, this one was filled with excitement.

We arrived at the pickup spot, waited briefly, and then the Jeeps began to arrive. We were split up into different vehicles, and I ended up in the first Jeep—the one leading out the entire brigade. No matter how tight the squeeze was, none of us cared. We were on our way to Israel, finally leaving Gaza for the last time. Within twenty-five minutes, we crossed the border and arrived at our destination. We were out of Gaza, and for me, this meant something even bigger: I was finishing my service and being released from the IDF.

Arriving at a field next to Gaza, we were filled with excitement. It was here in a large tent that we'd spend the night, and in the morning head to base. With a large barbecue, dancing, and smiles, everyone was having a good time. I took some food, looked around, and it hit me. I couldn't believe my time in the IDF was coming to an end, and if I was honest, a huge sense of guilt came over me. Since the start of the war, I'd told myself that I wasn't finishing until Omer was home. Now, while I knew the time was right to complete my military service because my battalion was no longer operating inside of Gaza, I felt guilty for leaving.

Beyond the guilt, I also was sad. Despite the difficulty of war, I knew I'd miss it. Fighting with my friends for something bigger than ourselves had given me meaning that I had never felt before. For everything to come to an end just like that wasn't easy. I knew I'd miss the army, and watching everyone celebrate in the open field only proved that to me.

The next day, before heading to base, the entire Paratrooper Brigade gathered for a huge ceremony marking an end to this chapter of the war. The ceremony was followed by an elaborate meal where I had steak on steak on steak. After this we headed to base for one night, and the following morning, Friday, March 1, we were released for a week at home. After that, I knew what was coming, and I was looking forward to it: my release from the IDF.

CHAPTER 14

LIFE IN GAZA

Gaza, November 4, 2023–February 28, 2024

One day in December 2023, my team went on an operation in Shejaiya. That night, though, the main focus wasn't the operation—it was the *main event*. I, Ira Kohler, the only non-Israeli on my team, was set to face another soldier in a rap battle. The opening ceremony was scheduled for 6:30 p.m., and after brief introductions, the battle would begin. We each had three rounds of prepared raps, and the contest had few, if any, rules.

Throughout the day, I prepared my raps. I sat for hours, thinking of clever rhymes and disses that would make the crowd go wild. A few days earlier, while my team was bored out of our minds, some of us had started joking around with rap-style jabs at one another. These spontaneous sessions quickly became more serious. We began preparing for proper rap battles, turning what started as a simple way to pass the time into a central team activity.

Although I was American and undoubtedly the worst Hebrew speaker in the group, I surprised myself by being pretty good at writing raps. During one of our early sessions, I came up with a jab so clever that it grabbed everyone's attention. When we decided to organize "official" battles, I was the first chosen. I faced off against a friend, and we both delivered raps at a level that should've turned me into the Jewish Kendrick Lamar.

Picture a room full of soldiers in a house in the middle of Gaza at night, illuminated only by a few red flashlights. Two guys stood in the center, trading jaw-dropping verses, while the crowd erupted after each line, trying to stay contained because, after all, we were still in Gaza. Given the group's dynamic, there were no boundaries. For that reason, I won't share the specific raps here, but after that iconic battle, the stage was set for nightly contests.

The contestants changed, but the atmosphere stayed the same. I quickly gained a reputation as one of the best, and someone asked me, "Ira, why don't you write a little rap about each person?"

I took the challenge seriously. After a long day of writing, I performed my personalized raps that night, each one packed with inside jokes and references to what each person was known for on the team. The group loved it, debating afterward which rap was the best and who got burned the most. For that brief period, I felt like a rap god.

Not every day in Gaza involved a mission or anything of real significance. Many days, we sat in a house, waiting for time to pass. We rotated guard duty, and to pass the time, we played card games or *shesh besh* (backgammon), exercised, cooked, and, of course, came up with creative distractions like the rap battles.

One day, a friend asked me about the United States, which led me to draw a massive map of America on the wall. Drawing on the walls had become its own activity. Several team members created murals that belonged in a museum, not a crumbling house in Gaza. I sketched the map from memory, complete with state lines. I managed to remember forty-nine of them, but the missing state nagged at me for hours. Without a phone or internet, I relied solely on my memory. My Israeli friends weren't much help; they only knew the obvious states like New York, Florida, and Texas. Finally, after hours of wracking my brain, I thought about the elections and watching John King on CNN on a November Tuesday evening. Finally, it hit me. The Iowa caucus! And yes, I know the Iowa caucus is for the primaries and not the general election, but that's how my brain worked. Iowa was the one I'd forgotten.

No sooner had I finished the map than another friend, a big NBA fan, challenged me to locate every NBA team. This task was easier than remembering the states, and I was able to mark all thirty teams, including the Toronto Raptors, and finished with the Detroit Pistons. The day had flown by, filled with the challenge of mapping states and teams.

Another favorite activity was the "interview." One day, a team-mate decided to interview another soldier. We turned it into a formal event, complete with strict rules: no laughing, smiling, or reacting to answers. The interviewer asked serious questions, and the interviewee had to respond seriously. Audience members could raise their hands to ask questions but were ejected if they broke the serious tone. Despite the humor of the setup, the interviews often led to deep, thought-provoking discussions. It was a rare opportunity to learn more about one another, beyond the usual banter. Each interview ended with the same question: If you could meet any person, dead or alive, who would it be?

Looking back, those moments of creativity and camaraderie helped us endure one of the hardest times of our lives. Whether through rap battles, maps, or interviews, we found ways to make the unbearable a little more bearable—and for that, I'll always be grateful.

Aside from these activities, there were other ways we passed the time, as well as routines we followed on a more consistent basis. I am often asked simple questions about my time in Gaza—questions not related to the war itself or anything operational, but rather about daily life. Where did you sleep? What did you eat? How did you get your food? What did you do in your downtime? Was there much downtime? What did living in Gaza look like?

What all of these questions have in common is that they aren't about fighting a war but about living in one. This section addresses those questions. Rather than focusing on what war looks like, I want to share what life in war looks like.

Food and Water

My introduction to army tuna was back in the early days of my service. A few days after I enlisted into the paratrooper unit, I found myself knee-deep in sand as I was trying out for Sayeret Tzanhanim, the special forces battalion of the Paratrooper Brigade.

This tryout wasn't like anything I had done before. In order to be accepted into the Paratrooper Brigade, I had to pass a tryout lasting no more than half a day, and only two hours of physical tests, as I described earlier in the book. This tryout was different. Called *gibbush yechatiyot*, it lasted three days, with hours upon hours of physical, mental, and social challenges.

The idea was to push us so hard that we'd reach our limits. Only at this point could the distinction between participants really show. I'll be honest, my performance wasn't the greatest. Physically, I dominated. It would be the social and mental components of the tryout that would challenge me most, and not knowing Hebrew to the level of my peers, I was already a step behind.

At one point during the tryout, we were given a box filled with cans. The guys next to me kept saying "*Manakim*; look, guys, we've finally made it to *Manakim*" with a half-smile and a small look of *ugh* on their faces. *Manakim* is an acronym for *manat krav* or, in English, "battle portion" or "battle ration," the typical food soldiers are given on the battlefield. Each box contains tuna, corn, beans, olives, peas, and, occasionally, mangos, halva, and chocolate spread—each in a can.

I was thrown a can of tuna and a can opener: *"Achi* (brother), can you open this?" I took the can of tuna, and now I was presented with a challenge. On Long Island I grew up with an electric can opener, not a flimsy little one like this. If you applied too much pressure on it while opening the can, the metal would bend, and there goes your can opener. A guy in our group saw me struggling and came over to help. This was all in the middle of the tryout, and while we were technically on a break, the judges were always watching. Seeing me struggling to open a can was probably not a good look. On the flip side, seeing another guy help was probably a good look for him. Is the reason why I didn't pass the tryout, because I couldn't open a can of tuna fish? I will never know for sure, but I have my suspicions!

With the can opened, I had my first bite of army tuna, but with time I would understand its significance within army culture. I soon learned the upgrade to army tuna was smoked tuna, and making smoked tuna is a pretty simple yet hotly debated procedure. The first step is to open the can, and as you can see from the story above, that might be the hardest step of all. The next step is to wisely choose the location you place the tuna. It's important that the area is secure and not exposed to the wind (you don't want the wind to blow out the flame), and it's important the can is not placed near anything flammable. You need to take out a roll of toilet paper and rip off approximately four squares. This could be controversial, but four is pretty standard. Folding the squares one on top of the other until you have one thick square, the toilet paper is placed on the oil lying above the tuna itself until it gets a bit wet but not completely soggy. Then, take a lighter and light the edges of the toilet paper on fire until a big flame appears over the can.

The next step is where the controversy begins: the waiting game. Exactly how long one waits before eating the tuna is the modern-day army Talmudic debate. Some would say that one must let the fire burn until it goes out by itself. With this method, one waits approximately forty-five minutes until there is no oil left. While this method is popular, to me, it is the less desirable option. With this method there is a benefit and a drawback. The benefit is that the top gets crispy; the drawback is that the tuna is dry.

My method is quicker and tastier. I let the tuna cook for roughly twenty to twenty-five minutes, or until the major flame subsides. While the top doesn't get as crispy, the tuna stays moist and smoky, exactly to my liking.

As you might now realize, army tuna or, more specifically, smoked tuna, was an essential part of our diet during the war in Gaza. While *manakim* consists of the typical army rations, and what we were given during many of our War Weeks during training, the food we were given throughout the real war was, to a degree, higher. Not anything gourmet, but we weren't eating entirely out of cans.

Before entering Gaza, we were each given a bag of food, or as we called them, *sakiot ochel*. Inside the bag was about a day's worth of food, but we were told that, in the worst case scenario, it should last up to forty-eight hours. Inside, naturally, was tuna. Usually one or two cans, depending on how lucky we got. Additionally, we had *kabanosim*, which are Slim Jims or dried hot dogs, a six-pack of bread rolls, protein bars, Nature Valley bars, a fruity bar, gum, Mentos, and, sometimes, an added treat.

Our company was given additional *sakiot ochel*, and we would divide the contents among the group. You might get an extra can of tuna, extra rolls, or extra *kabanosim*. In this way, we always brought more than the minimum.

In the early weeks of the war in Gaza, our mindset, that of our brigade, and of the army as a whole, was very limited when it came to food. We were learning how to fight this war but also how to live in this war. As time went on, the amount of food we were given started to increase, and the process of transporting food into the Gaza Strip became more routine.

The types of food we were given also started to improve. In addition to tuna, bread rolls, and *kabanosim*, we were given boxes of ramen noodles, tortillas, pasta, rice, sauces/spices, and other goodies as well. After all, most of our time was spent in the homes of Gazans, with gas stoves. While the electricity was out and the water wasn't running, we were still able to hook up gas tanks to the stove to allow us to cook.

So, we now had a kitchen, and our meals improved even more. The first step with a Jewish army (the only one in the world) was to kasher the cooking wear. Thankfully, that knowledge was plentiful. Friends on my team would first kasher all the pans, pots, silverware, and the like. (Not everyone in the IDF kept kosher in their everyday life, but we made sure we did in all our houses, so things were comfortable for all the men.) Once finished, the kitchen was ready for our use.

We would cook pasta and rice almost every day. Additionally, we would take those *kabanosim* or dried hot dogs, cut them up, and then sauté them in a pan. Put in some spices and sauces, mix the hot dogs with the rice, and you have a meal I would even eat in New York. I am not exaggerating. We would take ramen noodles, boil water, and cook the noodles, then we would sauté them in a pan with some spices, and you would have another meal. No longer were we eating a dried hot dog on a roll, but rather a much improved version. We took the television show *Chopped*, where a contestant has to make the best dish possible with the ingredients they are given, and turned our situation in Gaza into winning dishes.

With a stove, our mornings now started the way everyone starts their morning…with coffee. For us, it started the way many Israelis start their morning…with black Turkish coffee. Every morning, whoever was up first would get the water boiling on the stove and begin preparing the pot. In time I learned how to prepare the perfect cup. I'm not a coffee drinker; I love the taste, but I don't want to become addicted or reliant on caffeine. Nonetheless, the morning cup of black Turkish coffee would hit hard, and it became part of my routine. Considering I wasn't smoking cigarettes like most people on my team, drinking black coffee with them was a nice part of my day. Most of my friends would start their day with coffee in one hand and cigarette in the other…to them, the perfect way to start the morning.

My diet in Gaza, while expanded and improved with the use of a stovetop, doesn't really represent the true extent of how good our food really got, and that's because I am leaving out an important detail…the donations.

Israelis and Jews worldwide donated loads of food to IDF soldiers, both those inside the Gaza Strip and those outside. Occasionally we were given special foods, and these always served as the biggest treats. One of the greatest ones was when we were given a huge block of cheese and a grater. We made pasta with grated cheese on top as if we were in some fancy Italian restaurant, and one of our commanders even cooked a huge pot of rosetta for us all one night.

One day we woke up to the ultimate surprise: "Everyone is getting a McDonald's meal." *What?* I thought to myself. *Where am I?* Was there an Uber Eats driver delivering me a McDonald's Happy Meal inside Gaza? In fact, there was, and I couldn't believe it. It wasn't necessarily a Happy Meal, but rather a regular McDonald's burger, but I thought this was hilarious.

The most ironic part of this situation was that—and I am not lying when I say this—this was my first time ever eating McDonald's. I grew up keeping kosher in New York, and McDonald's isn't kosher. The only place to find a kosher McDonald's is in Israel, and to be honest, the establishment never attracted me. Now, in Gaza, with a McDonald's burger delivered to my doorstep, I said the *schechiyanu* and wolfed down a burger. It was cold and soggy because it had been traveling all day, so I couldn't give it a fair rating. Nonetheless, a burger in Gaza tasted amazing; who thought I'd ever eat a kosher McDonald's burger in Gaza?

While the big block of cheese and the McDonald's burger were nice, the best food we received came every week on Friday afternoon, just as Shabbat was about to begin. We would receive homemade cakes and challahs, pastries from bakeries, cans of soda or other soft drinks, random treats, and, finally, a home-cooked meal, consisting of chicken, meat, vegetables, potatoes, rice, and whatever else you would eat at your own Shabbat table. The idea, one that I love and that I think speaks to a core value within the IDF, is making Shabbat different from the rest of the week, even on a battlefield during a war.

We always looked forward to Shabbat meals, and it would usually be the one meal throughout the week when we would eat together, adding to the uniqueness of the meal and of Shabbat in general.

So, we had no lack of food in Gaza. While some days might be more limited than others, we always had enough to eat, and at many points, a variety of options. However, one of the most essential parts of our diet was water.

Whenever we entered Gaza, we had to bring at least six liters of water each, which is standard IDF practice. This didn't mean we shouldn't bring more, and I usually either carried 7.5 liters or even 9 to be safe. I didn't want to be wary of how much water I drank but rather have the ability to drink as I wished. We always received more water every day, so we never ran out. And, clearly, to cook rice and pasta, water is needed.

In time, the amount of water we received increased, allowing us to have a proper amount both to drink and to use for cooking.

While there was no running water in the houses in Gaza, there were several homes with huge water tanks. In these situations, we would take the opportunity to wash ourselves and clean our hands when necessary. The drinking water we received came from Israel in bottles, and that was also the water we used for cooking.

I'm sure you've been wondering, since I keep mentioning that we received food and water while in Gaza, exactly how we got the food and water. One of the new concepts I learned during the war is that of Malam, or replenishments. This means exactly what you'd think…a replenishment of whatever we needed. As we operated in different areas of Gaza, roads were established for military purposes connecting our position in Gaza to a point along the border. We called these roads two things: evacuation routes and logistic roads. In the case of an emergency, an IDF vehicle can quickly evacuate a wounded soldier to Israel using these routes, and from there, depending on the severity of their injury, they can be airlifted to a hospital. These roads became crucial for the IDF, and there were always soldiers dispersed along the road protecting it from terrorists. In fact, we spent many days inside Gaza not doing any actual fighting but rather positioning ourselves along these roads to protect them and allow IDF vehicles to drive safely by.

The other use for these roads, and the more common one, was for logistical purposes. Now, going back to the concept of Malam, on average we would receive replenishments every day. These replenishments went beyond food and water, as we received other things as well, but the most important thing was making sure we were well hydrated and had full stomachs.

So, there you have it. Our food situation in Gaza wasn't too bad after all. While we were not sitting at some fancy restaurant eating with cutlery, smoked tuna, the occasional treats, and the weekly Shabbat feasts were all we needed. We learned not only how to fight a war but such nourishment enabled us to learn how to live in one as well.

Accommodations

Throughout my IDF service, my grandma—Savta Syl—visited Israel twice. During those visits, I saw her on my days off when I could leave my base and meet her in some of the nicest hotels along the Tel Aviv beach, which had incredible views of the Mediterranean and, best of all, a lavish Israeli breakfast spread each morning: cheeses, salads, fish, *shakshuka*, pastries, fresh bread, and so much more.

The day after visiting Savta Syl, I usually found myself back on base—the same IDF outpost I had left just a couple of days earlier. The conditions there, let's just say, did not measure up to the Hilton. Still, we managed. I had never been one to complain about army conditions because, for the most part, I knew exactly what I had signed up for. If I had paid Hilton prices and received an IDF outpost, sure, I'd be furious. But I wasn't that out of touch with reality. Maybe my years at summer camp helped, but the often tight and grimy army conditions never really fazed me.

Heading into Gaza, however, I truly didn't know what to expect. Since this section is about living in a war rather than fighting in one, it makes sense to focus on the basics: where and how we lived.

Surprisingly, though I did spend a few nights sleeping outside under the stars—and rockets—most nights were spent under a roof. As I described earlier, the Gazan homes became our homes. Their kitchens became our kitchens. Their couches, our couches. Their beds, our beds. Their blankets and pillows, ours too. And yes, while it might sound gross at first, when you're already covered in sweat and dust, you'd rather have a pillow than not.

Essentially, once we cleared a new area, our forces would fill it. Each team took over a building or floor and transformed it into our home for however long we stayed. That could range from a single night to several weeks. We often had some idea of the duration, but it was never exact.

Once commanders selected our new home, we got to work making it livable. First, we divided the space into functional areas: a kitchen, a living room, a place for equipment, and sleeping quarters. We also had to designate spaces for specific needs: Where would we keep the shared food? Where could we work out? Which was the designated smoking area? Yes, IDF soldiers love to smoke cigarettes, if that wasn't clear already.

We split into teams, each with a job. After scanning the house, commanders assigned sleeping rooms. For safety, we always chose rooms farthest from the threat. For example, if we were advancing west, the cleared area would be to the east. That meant we chose east-facing rooms for sleep, because the west could still hold terrorists. Waking up to a threat in midsleep was a soldier's worst moment of vulnerability, and distance gave us some buffer.

To prepare sleeping rooms, we removed anything unnecessary—wardrobes, desks, nightstands, extra furniture. Then we gathered mattresses from around the house and arranged them tightly in a pattern that fit everyone. Usually, we needed two rooms for sleeping to fit our entire team. Every mattress got a blanket and pillow, and once we were set, we each marked our space by writing our initials on the wall above our mattress. From that point on, that was our bed. I always looked for one with a bit of space on either side for myself.

Next came the living space and equipment area. The living room just needed tidying up and enough seats for the team to hang out. If there weren't enough couches, we carried more up from other floors. We'd arrange everything—tables, chairs, couches—into a decent hangout spot.

The equipment area, though simple, was crucial. Commanders insisted we keep all gear together so, in an emergency, we'd all know exactly where to run. We arranged our bags in the shape of the Hebrew letter *chet*—as mentioned previously, a common formation in the IDF. In the middle of the *chet*, we placed a table with shared gear: cleaning supplies for weapons, extra tape and string, and other random tools.

The kitchen was the toughest to prepare. We cleaned it thoroughly and kashered all the cookware. Once ready, we stored our shared food, organized supplies, and brought in replacement gas tanks from other apartments for the burners. Cleanliness mattered, and in a Jewish army, kashrut was just as important.

The most important part of setting up the house, though, was making it operationally secure. Everything else—beds, kitchen, couches—was for comfort. But safety was life or death.

Each house required at least two soldiers to be on guard at all times, sometimes three, depending on the situation. At every location, we assigned a soldier to sit near the stairwell and monitor that entry. That post, the "defensive post," was our first and last line of defense. The other guard stations were "offensive posts"—they monitored exposed directions. If the area west of us hadn't been cleared yet, we placed a guard facing west. Instead of windows—which were obvious targets—we made small holes in walls to watch through. A soldier would sit quietly and keep watch. These guard positions had to be both operational and bearable, since someone sat there for an hour at a time.

With no electricity, we relied on flashlights—and only the red-light setting at night. Red light traveled less than white, making it harder for enemies to detect. To keep the light contained, we also had to cover every window. Using nails and hammers, we sealed windows with blankets, curtains, or rugs—whatever we could find. It wasn't enough to just hang them up. We nailed them down on all corners to block every sliver of light. This had to be done in every room: kitchen, bedrooms, bathrooms, everywhere. And when a nail came loose, or a blast shook one down, we fixed it immediately.

As you might imagine, these sealed homes became suffocating hot boxes. Add in the cigarette smoke from half the team and the stench became a permanent resident. During daylight, we opened windows for air—never on the threat-facing side, of course—but it made a difference.

We did our best to make things livable. If we stayed in one place for more than a few days, we did daily *misdarim*—team cleanups. We rotated tasks: tidying, sweeping, refastening window covers. The kitchen was always the hardest. It got messy fast, and we had to throw out expired food to avoid attracting pests.

Our accommodations were never luxurious—but they were the best we could make of what we had. Living in Gazan homes gave us a glimpse into what life there might have been like before the war. Still, transforming those homes into something functional and secure was our focus, both for comfort and survival.

Exercise

One of my favorite parts of the army, oddly enough, was the classic Bar-Or, the IDF fitness exam. It had a few components, like pull-ups and dips, but the main event—the one everyone cared about—was the three-kilometer run. For me, it was a chance to shine. When it came to other parts of training—gun knowledge, field exercises, even conversations in Hebrew—I always felt a step behind. A lot of Israelis grew up around guns or in youth programs that taught them army basics. My first interaction with a weapon was in the IDF. But physical fitness was my thing. I usually scored toward the top of my team.

Fitness is taken seriously in the IDF, especially in combat units. There's pressure to train beforehand just to be ready for the physical toll on your body. Once you're in, your body is reshaped to meet the demands of a combat soldier. We weren't hitting the gym like bodybuilders to sculpt abs or biceps. That stuff didn't really matter. Sure, we would hold a plank long enough to question our life choices, but the priority was functional strength. Strength to carry heavy weights across long distances.

That kind of training defined our routine. I lost count of how many times I marched five, ten, or even fifteen kilometers straight with nearly one hundred pounds of gear on me, simulating movements deep within enemy territory. These exercises were intense—and probably explain why I have issues with my back to this day.

We hit the gym when we could, especially once we finished training and were given a little more freedom. On our own time, we'd work out however we wanted. But when October 7th came, all of that stopped.

Obviously, while fighting in Kibbutz Be'eri, fitness routines weren't on our minds. But even in the weeks that followed—while we prepared to enter Gaza—working out was the last thing we cared about. We had just witnessed a massacre against our people and were heading into a war zone. The idea of doing bicep curls or core workouts felt absurd. And for the first few months in Gaza, the motivation still wasn't there.

Eventually, though, things shifted. As our food situation improved, and as it became clear this war wasn't ending anytime soon, we started to realize that not moving and exercising was hurting us. Don't get me wrong—there were still plenty of days we were operating inside Gaza, using our bodies nonstop. But there were also long stretches when we were just sitting inside some Gazan house, doing nothing, barely moving.

In early January, when we were stationed in El Bureij in Central Gaza, some of us started easing back into workouts. We'd do push-ups, planks, tricep dips—basic bodyweight stuff. But we also got creative.

For added weight, we'd lift six-packs of water or even our guns. My gun weighed about 7.6 kilograms. Add a full ammo belt—around 150 bullets—and it came out to 10.5 kilograms. That's over twenty pounds. Perfect for bicep curls. If a house had a ledge, we'd do pull-ups. We made it work.

A few weeks later, as we were moving into Khan Yunis for the first time, one of my teammates—who's obsessed with fitness, and even studying to be a personal trainer in his post-IDF life—brought actual exercise equipment with him. Alongside our weapons, he carried in exercise bands, a TRX set, and even a pull-up bar that could hook onto a doorframe. So now, in the middle of Gaza, we had a whole setup. We still used guns as weights (because why wouldn't we?), but now we had more variety.

These workouts did more than just help us stay in shape. They gave us structure. They gave us something to do during the long, dull hours sitting around in some random Gazan's home. And more than anything, they gave us a brief moment of normalcy in a place that was anything but. It became something I looked forward to every day—and it always made me feel better.

Living

A major theme of life in Gaza is the level of creativity we used. And I don't mean just regular creativity, but rather Israeli creativity. And, for anyone who knows, Israeli creativity comes with its own uniqueness.

As I said, workouts became an important part of our routine. They allowed us to pass the time, get stronger, and provide a sense of normalcy. However, after that, we would stink, and a shower was necessary. But… the fact that we stunk was not the issue—after all, we weren't attending a wedding, going on a first date, or interviewing at Morgan Stanley. Our situation, clearly, didn't lend itself to a fresh, clean cologne smell.

We all stank, and there was nothing to do about it. The intention behind our "baths" were solely for hygienic purposes, and not really much else. Staying clean and healthy was the priority, not smelling good.

Rather than creating a bubble bath in which to bathe, we would reach into our bags and pull out one of the most important items for any combat soldier: baby wipes. We would take out a few, rub our bodies, rub our feet and in between our toes, rub down there, if you know what I mean, and give some baby wipes to a friend, who would rub our backs. If any of this is too graphic, you can skip forward several paragraphs. When that was done, we would take out the second most important item for any combat soldier: baby powder. To keep dry and avoid chafing, after washing our body with these wipes, we would pat ourselves down with this powder: from our feet, to our backs, to, yes, down there again. After this process we might not smell like a million bucks, but we certainly felt like them. Occasionally during these cleaning sessions, we would also change clothes, but that was rare.

This idea of hygiene extended far beyond our baby-wipes-and-baby-powder cleaning sessions. Like I said, hygiene was very important, and we made sure to prioritize it. Every morning and night I would brush my teeth. If my mother, who is a dentist, found out that I wasn't brushing twice a day, she would have killed me sooner than any terrorist would.

Another important aspect of our hygienic routine was the use of hand sanitizer. Life in Gaza is filthy, and one just has to touch a wall to feel that. There were no places to wash our hands before diving into smoked tuna, and I always found myself squirting a drop of hand sanitizer into my palms. We'd also find time to cut our nails, wash our faces with water, and monitor our temperature. If, at any point, someone was feeling sick, they would be seen by a medic and given the proper medical attention. In short, health and hygiene became important parts of our routine, which I think was widely overlooked from an outsider's perspective. But, certainly, Hamas can't be defeated by a bunch of sick soldiers.

Beyond our health and hygiene, life in Gaza brought its challenges but also its smiles. As I mentioned earlier, we had many fun and funny times. This goes from the rap battles and interviews to the everyday games and shenanigans.

Just as any family might sit around on a Friday night playing board games, so did we. Shesh besh, or backgammon, became one of my favorites. This game is a classic in Israeli society. We would sit with our black Turkish coffee in hand and play game after game, and I got pretty good at it.

The games we played, however, went far beyond Shesh besh. We would play chess, checkers, and a multitude of different card games. And, during the November 2023 weeklong ceasefire, while stationed in Gaza, we were brought a whole slew of additional board games for our pleasure.

Beyond the games we'd play together, there were other activities that helped pass the time, and one of those was reading books. Every time we were preparing to reenter Gaza, we were given many books to choose from. Like searching through a library, my friends would rifle through the books, deciding what was worth bringing and what wasn't. Unfortunately for me, all the books were in Hebrew, and I didn't have the bandwidth to think so hard while reading. I decided at one point to bring a book of mine from home, and in addition to that, a friend on my team who was originally from the United States, brought in a Kindle with English books, and from time to time I would take the device and read a little.

Another important way we passed the time was listening to music. Many of my friends brought MP3 players with downloaded music into Gaza. Ironically, in 2023, way beyond the days of MP3s, this war brought them back into style. One evening in Khan Yunis, a friend came to me as I was deep into a book I brought from home, and he said I had received a package. And I know what you're thinking, a package? The Israeli postal service is slower than a turtle, yet you received packages in Gaza? Yes, that is correct. Parents and friends could bring packages to soldiers on our base, and from there they would be brought into Gaza.

I started opening the box and inside was an MP3 player, with a note from my summer camp, Young Judaea Sprout Lake, which had become a home away from home for me, both as a camper and as staff for many years. Because I was operating many months in the war, they wanted to send me a little treat, and the gift was beyond appreciated. In addition to music, the MP3 also gave me access to the radio, making listening to the news a lot easier. And, most meaningful of all, they downloaded several camp songs onto the MP3 so that I could plug in earphones and listen to the same tunes I grew up singing at camp. Truly a special gift.

While the war brought back the MP3, that wasn't the only thing that came back in style. In a time when everyone has an Apple or Android phone, this war brought back the classic flip phone. A phone, shockingly, that did nothing more than make calls. While we couldn't bring our regular phones into Gaza, many in my company brought flip phones as a way to call home. Heading to the top of a building to try to get a signal, we would call home every so often. This ended up being a pretty comical affair. The signal was never too great, and often I'd find soldiers, myself included, walking around on the top floor of a building trying to find some spotty signal. When one found the right spot—let's call it the sweet spot—that spot became everyone's go-to. Taking turns, soldiers would stand in that exact location, not moving so as not to disrupt the connection, and call home.

Wanting to stay on a routine, I decided to give my parents a call twice a week, once on Tuesdays and a second time on Fridays right before

Shabbat. Frankly, I didn't want to share much; I was more interested in hearing what was happening at home. And keeping to a Tuesday/Friday routine gave my parents a sense of ease because they would expect a call on those days and wouldn't be worried about hearing from me.

With all of this said, the real way we passed the time was simply by sitting around, talking and relaxing with one another. The worst part for me was the smoking. We designated one area of the house to be the smoke area, and this was always the living room. As we sat, at least a third of my team would have a cigarette in hand. For me, completely disgusted by the smell, I found even sitting in the area suffocating. Nonetheless, I would make do because I enjoyed being with my team.

We would sit together for hours on end, talking about the most random things, laughing, joking, and getting to know one another. It was really in these situations, more than anything else, that I learned about my team and grew closer to them.

Life in Gaza had its uniqueness and its sense of normalcy. The final thing, and something I can't not mention, was how exactly we would use the restroom. If you want to skip this part, I won't be offended. Just fast forward to the next chapter.

The first, obviously, is number one. At first, with little experience in Gaza, we would go in the toilet itself. However, because we were in a war zone, the last thing present was a working plumbing system. When the urine lingered and wouldn't go down, it started to pick up a smell, and this wasn't going to go unnoticed for long. We started, then, to do two things. The first was to go in an empty bottle and then throw the bottle out the window. The outside, unfortunately, became our garbage. This wasn't to pollute the environment in any way, but for hygienic purposes, and because we had no other alternative, all waste was hurled outside a window, as far as possible from our living quarters.

The second way was to relieve ourselves down the sink. Unlike a toilet, the urine wouldn't linger but would go down the pipes. If we noticed that the sink started to smell, we would pour mouthwash, which we received in donations, down the sink to, theoretically, clean the affected area. Was this perfect? Certainly not. However, we preferred the smell of fresh mint over urine. However, let me be clear, this was not the same sink we used to brush our teeth and spit. We would choose one sink in the house for urine and the other for teeth. Whoever mixed up the two would certainly hear about it from the team!

While my focus has been on number one, I'm sure you're also wondering about number two. After all, it is something we all must do. Our approach was similar to our first method for dealing with number one. We accumulated many plastic bags, and whenever we had to go number two, we'd go to the bathroom furthest from our main living quarters, go in a plastic bag, and then hurl the bag outside as far away from us as possible. While, yes, this was disgusting, there was no alternative. Keeping the bags inside the house would be a nightmare and create an unsanitary environment for anyone, especially a soldier trying to stay healthy. This, I'm sure, is the real detail you were thinking about, never had the courage to ask, and now unfortunately know all about. You're welcome.

Life in Gaza, as opposed to fighting a war in Gaza, was unique and normal at the same time. From our living conditions to our food, from our hygienic routines to the ways we passed the time, there was a unique way to live life in a war. This way of life became routine as time went on, and there was an understanding that the luxuries of a bathroom, a full kitchen, or even a shower were eventually going to come back into our lives, but for now, while we fought a war, the best we could do was learn how to live in one, and I think we did quite well.

CHAPTER 15

OMER NEUTRA

Omer's Life, October 14, 2001–October 7, 2023

It takes a village to raise a child. In my early days in Israel, I watched the kids of Kibbutz Erez roam freely—biking, laughing, and exploring on their own. Parents trusted not just their children, but the community around them. The kibbutz wasn't just a neighborhood; it was home in the fullest sense. Children weren't raised by a household, but by a village. Watching life unfold in Erez, I couldn't help but reflect on the place I had come from—my own slice of community, back in the United States. Like the kibbutz, it wasn't the walls of my house that defined home—it was the people. My parents intentionally built our lives among those who shared our values: Judaism, family, community, and purpose.

We were raised in a world where Judaism wasn't merely something we believed, but something we lived. Israel wasn't just a faraway concept; it was part of who we were. Our community measured wealth not in material things, but in love, friendship, and connection. No matter how long you were gone, you could always return and be embraced.

But unlike in Israel, Jewish life in the US requires deliberate effort.

My parents grounded us in institutions that reflected our values. They chose the Schechter School of Long Island for our education, even with the steep cost of tuition, because they wanted us raised in a space that nurtured Jewish identity. Year after year, I returned to a school that taught Torah, Hebrew, Jewish holidays, and—most of all—belonging. We joked that we were "Schechter blessed," not for academics, but for the friendships and the community that surrounded us.

Our community wasn't homogenous—families differed in observance and views—but our shared values united us. Together, we built something greater than ourselves: a Jewish life defined not just by faith or practice, but by people who showed up for one another.

Less than a ten-minute drive from our house on Long Island lived a beautiful family—the Neutras. What made the Neutra family unique, at least in our eyes, was one simple fact: The parents, Orna and Ronen, were Israeli. After moving to the United States, they decided to plant roots and raise a family in the same Jewish community my family had chosen.

A few weeks after 9/11, Orna gave birth to their first son, Omer, followed a few years later by his younger brother, Daniel. With their rapid-fire Hebrew conversations and that signature edge of tough Israeliness, there was always something distinctly different about the Neutras. They were part of a tight-knit group of Israeli families on Long Island—a community that came with a high barrier to entry. If you could sit around the table and speak Hebrew, you belonged. If not, well…you weren't exactly part of the club.

But Orna and Ronen didn't stop with just the Israeli crowd. They made a deliberate effort to give their kids a deeper sense of Jewish identity, one rooted in tradition, community, and connection to Israel—just as my own parents had. Omer and Daniel attended the Schechter School of Long Island for thirteen years, just like my siblings and me. Both families were members of Midway Jewish Center, and we all spent our summers at Young Judaea's Camp Sprout Lake.

Over time, the Neutras became one of the families closest to ours. We often had Shabbat dinners together. As we got older, Omer would take charge of the hummus, and this wasn't your average supermarket hummus. It was the real stuff—authentic, homemade, and bursting with the kind of flavor that lingered long after the meal was over.

Naturally, given our ages, Omer became the one I connected with the most. We spent plenty of time at each other's houses, usually playing basketball out front. He had the height advantage, but I had the skill— and our games were always tight. In the summers, my siblings and I would head to their house to swim in the pool, shoot hoops, or play ping-pong. But the highlight of it all was always the food. With every visit, the Neutra house gave me a taste of Israel.

In the simplest of terms, Omer and I were childhood friends.

As the years went on, our friendship evolved. We no longer hung out at each other's houses as often, but we remained close—always friends in school and within our community. Omer became very involved in USY, the Conservative Movement's youth group, eventually serving as president of the Long Island division, and later, of the entire New York Metropolitan region. Leadership came naturally to Omer. He had a platform to showcase his skills and built a strong, loyal community of friends within USY.

But his leadership didn't stop there. Omer was also involved in the local Israeli Scouts, and within our school he captained several sports teams—dominating the court in both basketball and volleyball. Despite his achievements, Omer remained humble. He listened. He cared for those who felt left behind. And because we lived in the same community, our bond remained strong.

I was a year older than Omer. I graduated from high school in 2018 and went off to college, and naturally, our paths drifted apart a bit. Omer was still in school, and I'd only see him during occasional visits home—usually around a Shabbat dinner table. I distinctly remember visiting our high school during Thanksgiving break of my freshman year in college. Omer was a senior at the time. As I walked the familiar halls, peeking into classrooms to find friends or old teachers, I reached a room at the end of the hall. The teacher noticed me, offered a quick smile and a small embrace, not wanting to interrupt the lesson. Then Omer spotted me. Our eyes locked, and before I knew it, he was calling me into the classroom. The lesson came to a pause as he got up and gave me a big bear hug—the kind that was so quintessentially Omer.

Not long after that, I returned to college, and time passed. After graduating high school, Omer chose to spend a year at a *mechina*, a pre-IDF gap year program in Israel called Mechinat Galil Elyon. He had already been accepted to Binghamton University and deferred his studies to explore Israel. But in truth, it wasn't Israel he was exploring—Omer already knew Israel. He had family there. He'd spent time there. This year was about something deeper: It was Omer's chance to explore himself.

Living alongside Israelis preparing for military service, Omer faced a decision. Should he finish the year and return to the US to start college, or should he continue down the path his Israeli peers were taking and enlist in the IDF? To make a long story short—and since we already know the answer—Omer chose the latter.

By the time Omer was starting his army journey, I was a year away from graduating college myself. What most people didn't know then was that I, too, had been planning to enlist in the IDF once I finished my degree.

And so, there we were. Two boys from the same town and the same community. Shaped by the same values, wearing the same uniform, standing side by side in defense of our country and our people. The connection between Omer and me had taken on a new meaning—one that was different from any other relationship I had. He was the only person who truly understood where I came from, who could say he knew the world I grew up in, and who, like me, now strapped on boots and held a rifle in defense of something far greater than ourselves.

Omer enlisted into Shiryon, the IDF's tank unit, and served with immense pride. He completed his training, became a commander and, later, an officer. My parents and I even had the honor of attending his commander's ceremony, as his parents weren't able to fly in from the United States. But Omer was far from alone—his large Israeli family filled the crowd, and there was no shortage of proud supporters cheering him on that day.

While Omer was deep into his service, I was just beginning. After graduating college and moving to Israel, I enlisted in the IDF and began at the Hebrew course on the Michve Alon base. The environment there was unlike anything I'd ever experienced—a melting pot of soldiers from across the globe. I found myself interacting with people from South America, Ukraine, Russia, France, and, of course, other English speakers like myself. The diversity was eye-opening and, at times, overwhelming.

This was my first real taste of the IDF's rough edges—its bluntness, its intensity, its chaos. I was slowly learning how to swim in a sea I had only read about, a system I'd only ever idealized. My ideological love for Israel, my belief in the importance of defending the Jewish state, had brought me here. The principle that if all Israelis serve, why shouldn't I?—that's what landed me in uniform. It was my upbringing, the values I grew up with, the community that shaped me—all of it brought me to this dirt, these boots, this base. And I knew Omer had come from the same place, rooted in the same values.

But then I'd overhear conversations—soldiers talking about why they wanted to join a combat unit. Most were passionate about Israel, sure. But others talked about their love of guns, the thrill of looking tough, or even worse, revenge against those who hated Israel. That shook me. While I recognized that everyone comes to the army with different backgrounds and motivations—and, yes, any reason to defend your country is valid—some of these sentiments felt far removed from the idealism that had brought me there.

And beyond ideology, the culture itself could be downright wild. Not everyone, of course—there were plenty of levelheaded, motivated men. But the chaos still stood out. I remember one moment in particular: a full-on brawl between the French- and Arab-speaking soldiers that erupted over a yogurt cup. A yogurt cup! It felt like something straight out of a public school cafeteria in a movie from the 1980s.

One night, just a few weeks into my service, I called my parents. I was overwhelmed, trying to make sense of it all. My mom said something simple but spot on: "I think you need to speak with Omer. He's the only one who'll really understand you."

And she was right.

I texted him, and we made plans to meet. On a Friday morning in the heart of winter, we found ourselves at a small café on Sheinkin Street in Tel Aviv. We both ordered *shakshuka*, and in between bites, we caught up. We talked about his service as a tank commander and my experience in the Hebrew course. We discussed which units I might end up in, and of course, we reminisced a bit about home.

I brought up the culture shock I was experiencing and asked if he had felt it too. Omer then said something I'll never forget: "Listen," he said. "Israelis are crazy. And Israeli soldiers? Even more. But the ones who aren't here for the right reasons don't last. When the army gets hard, and you're out of your Hebrew course and into the real stuff, the ones who really want to be here, those are the ones who'll stay. The rest?

They'll fade out. You won't have to worry about them."

And he was right. As my service went on and things got harder, I started to see it with my own eyes. The ones who stayed—the ones who pushed through the cold, the exhaustion, the fear—were the ones driven by something deeper. The values we came with, the ideals we held onto, they weren't just background noise. They were fuel.

Omer's message stuck with me long after that café breakfast. It reminded me to keep my head up, to keep going. It reminded me why I was there. Even in the toughest moments, his words echoed in the back of my mind: *remember why you're here*. Remember where you come from. Let your values carry you when nothing else can.

I remembered Omer's words—and from there, our service continued. I enlisted into the paratroopers, and Omer carried on as a tank commander. But in true Omer fashion, serving as a commander wasn't enough—naturally, he had to become an officer. Just another testament to his selflessness and bravery.

After eight grueling months, Omer completed his officer's course in February 2023. That was the last time I saw him.

Although I couldn't attend this ceremony in person as I had for his commander's course, my brother and I made sure to celebrate in our own way. The morning after, we visited Omer and his parents at their Airbnb in Tel Aviv. It was another beautiful winter morning, and this time we sat outside on their porch overlooking the Mediterranean Sea.

The Neutras had prepared a classic Israeli breakfast—the kind that reminded me of Shabbat meals back at their house on Long Island. As we sat together, we flipped through pictures on the television from the ceremony the day before. The pride on Orna and Ronen's faces was unmistakable.

That morning gave Omer a brief chance to rest and be with his family before stepping into his new role. And for me, it was back to my own unit, continuing my journey in the army.

As the months went on, we continued protecting the State of Israel. I spent several months stationed in Hebron, while Omer was based at the Tze'elim training base in the Negev. By July, our roles reversed. Omer left Tze'elim and was now stationed along the Gaza border, and I, in turn, left Hebron and was sent to the Nebi Musa training base for the next few months.

The next time both of us were scheduled to switch positions was four months later, in early November 2023. Omer was set to finish his time on the Gaza border, and I was scheduled to take his place, assigned to the Nahal Oz outpost.

But of course, none of that happened.

To this day, I often think about the alternative. What if October 7th had happened just one month later—say, on November 7th instead? Our stories could have been entirely different. Omer wouldn't have been there that horrible day. And there's a real chance that I would have.

On the morning of October 7, 2023, as I stood ready to board a helicopter into the unknown, Omer's fate was already unfolding.

That morning, Omer was serving with his men along the border. In the days leading up to the October 7th attack, the situation had been tense—Gazan protesters and rioters had stirred unrest, creating pressure and uncertainty for IDF forces. But on Friday night, October 6, things seemed to calm down. Omer called his mother and told her that, for the first time in a while, there was a sense of quiet, but because this was a Jewish holiday, Omer made sure his team remained on high alert while hoping that Shabbat would pass in peace.

We now know that didn't happen.

The next morning, the exact opposite of peace unfolded. At 6:29 a.m. on Saturday, October 7, 2023, Hamas breached the border, launching thousands of rockets into the sky and sending thousands of terrorists across the ground. IDF first responders rushed to the scene—and among the very first was Omer and his tank crew of Shaked Dahan, Oz Daniel, and Nimrod Cohen.

They raced to the border, and Omer ordered another tank that was with them to split off to cover more ground. After checking an opening in the fence, Omer's tank turned back around. Terrorists reached the tank and attached explosive charges at strategic points. The driver's compartment exploded, killing the driver, Shaked Dahan, instantly, and the tank caught fire. The crew attempted to rotate the tank to prevent terrorists from climbing onto it, but then Hamas fired an anti-tank missile, striking the turret and disabling the tank entirely.

The crew was stuck inside unable to breathe. Over the radio, Omer called for assistance. But help never came. Omer ordered his team to grab their guns and prepare for disembarkment. However, the crew was outnumbered by the terrorists waiting for them outside. As they opened the hatch, they were dragged out by an angry mob—beaten, kicked, and taken hostage into Gaza.

We now know that Omer was severely wounded or killed in these moments, and Oz was killed right after they escaped the tank. All crew members were taken into Gaza—only Nimrod survived the day and, two years later, returned alive to Israel.

Of course, at the time, we didn't know any of these details, and I had no idea this was happening at all. Disconnected from the outside world, we had no phones, no updates, no access to the horror that was unfolding around us. My fight against those very same terrorists stretched late into the night and continued in the days that followed.

We moved from Kibbutz Be'eri to Kibbutz Alumim, and then eventually to the paratroopers' training base, where we began preparing for what we now knew was coming: a war in Gaza.

The night we arrived at the paratrooper training base—October

15, more than a week after the October 7th attack—I finally reconnected with my personal phone for the first time. A flood of messages poured in. I skimmed through the news, trying to make sense of what was happening beyond what I had seen with my own eyes. The death toll, the injured, and of course—the number that shook me most—the hostage count: 251 hostages in Gaza. A crisis far greater than that of Gilad Shalit. A tragedy unlike anything Israel had ever faced before.

It never occurred to me that someone I knew personally could be among the killed or captured. I figured that by now, more than a week later, if something had happened to someone close to me, I would have known. Even without a phone, I believed that somehow—some way—word would have reached me.

But that night, the most important thing I did with my phone was call my family.

Now that I was reconnected with the outside world, with full access to my social media, my parents understood they could no longer shield me from the truth. During the days I was fighting, the last thing they wanted was to break the news that Omer had been taken hostage. But they knew it was better that I hear it from them, not read about it on Instagram.

So they told me—over the phone, gently but clearly: Omer was one of them. One of the 251. The details were still unfolding, but enough was confirmed. My childhood friend, Omer Neutra, was a hostage in Gaza.

The next few months, as the war in Gaza raged on, thoughts of Omer never left my mind. The dream of his return became my inspiration that, even in the darkest moments, pushed me to lock in and keep fighting. It brought me back to that breakfast in Tel Aviv where he told me to always remember the "why" behind my service. But what Omer didn't know was that the "why" had changed. I was no longer fighting just for my people and the protection of the State of Israel—now, I was fighting for my friend. This new purpose gave me a deeper motivation than ever before and more certainty in my will to carry on.

The months flew by, but there were no signs of Omer. Whenever I spoke with my parents, the first question I asked was always about him. They had no updates, and so I chose to let that hope—that spark of his return—continue to drive me forward. After finishing my required service, I decided to stay on for reserve duty. There was a voice in my head telling me that as long as Omer was still in Gaza, suffering underground, I needed to be there fighting for him.

Orna Neutra, Omer's mother, spoke to me on the phone and told me that if I was going to keep fighting in Gaza, it shouldn't be for her son. We didn't know if or when Omer would come home, and she didn't want me risking my life until that happened. I think, deep down, she feared that if something were to happen to me while trying to rescue her son, she would carry a burden of guilt.

Still, I continued my service, finally finishing for good in mid-March 2024. After over one hundred days in the Gaza Strip and surviving the intense fighting of October 7th, it was time to return my gun—a few months later than planned, but for me, at the right time.

The idea that Omer was still underground, while I was no longer fighting in Gaza, weighed heavily on me. I wanted to fight until the moment Omer could hug his parents again, but deep down, I knew I couldn't wait forever. And, heartbreakingly, I also knew that day might never come.

My fight shifted into a different form. Through my limited phone access over those past few months, I saw a whole other front emerging—a front fighting for Omer in a way no less important. The "Bring Them Home Now" movement had formed across Israel and around the world, demanding that every hostage be returned to their families, and that the fallen receive a proper burial. Even closer to home, in Plainview,

New York, a more personal movement arose: Bring Omer Home.

Between rotations in Gaza and calls with my parents, I witnessed the incredible efforts back home—in the very community where Omer and I grew up and that inspired us both to serve. After completing my IDF service, I found myself back on Long Island, surrounded by those fighting a different kind of battle. Every week, the local "Run for Their Lives" group marched through our town, holding posters of Omer and the other hostages—showing the world who was missing and demanding their safe return. I saw rallies, events, and speakers raising awareness about the hostage crisis. My community—without guns but with powerful voices—reported to duty with immense pride and passion.

The same families who shaped my upbringing, the same Jewish institutions that taught me so much, and the same community that made me who I am, now fought for Omer's release in a completely different way than I had. Without weapons, but with voices that could not be ignored.

For me, it all felt strange. It was Omer who had been my companion through it all. Though we weren't in the same unit or friend group in Israel, he was the one who understood me best. He knew where I came from, and in the hardest moments in a world so foreign, it was Omer who understood me. Now, after surviving October 7th and months of fighting in Gaza, I was home. But the other person who had started the journey with me—from the same place, with the same values—was still stuck.

More than ever, my motivation was at its peak. Though I no longer carried a machine gun around my shoulders, that weapon had transformed into a different kind of power—a voice. A voice to expose Hamas's atrocities and a voice to fight relentlessly for the release of my friend, held hostage by merciless killers.

For months, I spoke passionately about Omer. Sharing my October 7th story at synagogues, schools, and community gatherings, I always concluded by highlighting my personal connection to him—sharing his character and spirit with the world. My message was always clear: This fight isn't over until every last one of our people is safely home. I was privileged to speak at several rallies, shining a spotlight on Omer and emphasizing the urgent, ongoing hostage crisis.

"Bring Omer Home" grew into a movement that evolved and expanded far beyond our community. Orna and Ronen Neutra devoted nearly fourteen months to traveling the world—from the United States to Israel, Europe, and beyond—pouring every ounce of their strength into advocating for Omer's release. They appeared on nearly every American and Israeli news channel, sharing their son's story with the world. His younger brother Daniel stood by their side, holding a striking poster of Omer's face against a vivid red background—a contrast impossible to miss—as they pushed for action through interviews, rallies, and meetings with government officials.

Then one day, there came a knock on their door that changed everything. On the evening of Sunday, December 1, 2024, the Neutras were delivered news that shattered their world. On that dark day—October 7th—the day the Jewish people will never forget, and the day more Jews died than any since the Holocaust, the hero of Long Island, Omer Neutra, took his last breath at the hands of Hamas.

What no one could have known was that while his parents believed their son was trapped deep underground in Hamas's tunnels, unable to hear their voices, Omer was, in fact, watching from above. He witnessed his parents' tireless travels across the globe fighting for his release. He saw me and others fighting for him on the ground. He saw communities worldwide—and especially his own community on Long Island, the place that made him who he was—stand strong and fight for him. Omer watched as those who knew him grew to know him better, and those who never met him felt as if they knew him, and as if he knew them. It sounds almost magical, but there is something truly powerful about this shared connection.

For fourteen months, Omer's family and community fought tirelessly, sharing his story with the world. It's as if the world first had to come to know who Omer was before learning that he was no longer with us. And in that, the fight was worth it. In a way, as Omer's story reached the world, I felt as if my own story and values were being shared too. The world wasn't just learning about the soldier who fell that day—they were learning about everything that inspired that soldier to be who he was. The same things that inspired me.

After the news of Omer's passing, the fight changed but became no less important. As did the families of so many others taken hostage in Gaza, the Neutras and the Jewish people now fought for the return of his body, so that his family could give him a proper burial—a place to visit and call his final resting place.

The fight continued on, and as the community learned of his passing, they found beautiful and meaningful ways to commemorate Omer, his life, and his deep connection to the community that raised him.

Our local synagogue, Midway Jewish Center, raised funds to dedicate a Torah in Omer's honor—a beautiful way to commemorate him for generations to come. His camp, Sprout Lake, is building The Omer Neutra Center for Leadership, Israel, and Jewish Education in his memory. Nassau County, Long Island, chose to rename a street in his hometown of Plainview to Captain Omer Neutra Way, and the Town of Oyster Bay renamed a park in the neighborhood he grew up in as the Captain Omer Neutra Memorial Park. These tributes were a symbol of support from the broader, including non-Jewish, community. At the street-naming ceremony, Omer's brother Daniel called this new street sign a "sign of life," a powerful message after not having heard any news from Omer since the war began. Now, as locals pass by this road, they see this sign of life from Omer himself.

We waited, we prayed, and we fought. We fought for Omer to come back alive, and then we fought for the return of Omer's body. On Sunday, November 2, 2025, Hamas finally handed over the remains of Omer Neutra, and five days later, a funeral was held. Twenty-five months after Omer was killed, he was finally given the proper burial he deserved.

Omer Neutra's story is far from over—and, in truth, it will never be over. For me, Omer's story is the story of my community and the story of me: how a young boy from Long Island, raised with deep Jewish values and a love of Israel, chose to enlist in the IDF and defend its land. Omer's story is my story, and the only difference between us is that I'm here to write this book, to tell my story. And with that, to tell his story as well.

His story reflects a strong Jewish upbringing and a loving family grounded in timeless values. Omer's personality embodied leadership, kindness, unity, and sacrifice—qualities every parent hopes their child will have.

As time passes and the horror of October 7th becomes a more distant memory, Omer will stand as a symbol for generations—a man who did everything right and answered the call in one of our toughest moments. The responsibility of everyone fortunate enough to have known him is to ensure that Omer's story continues to inspire and live on for generations to come.

CHAPTER 16

POST SERVICE

Civilian Life, March 11, 2024–Present

There is a tradition in the IDF that when a soldier's mandatory service comes to an end, they stand before their friends with their *choger* in one hand and a pair of scissors in the other—and then they cut the card. For a mother of a combat soldier, this day is often more cherished than the day their child was born. That moment symbolizes the end of compulsory military service and the beginning of civilian life once again. Of course, especially during wartime, soldiers are often called back for reserve duty, but at least the hardest days of mandatory service are behind them.

Leading up to this release, there is a quirky practice called—no joke—*shigi-digi*. Essentially, *shigi-digi* is the process of learning how to speak civilian again, rather than military. Moving to Israel and improving my Hebrew wasn't enough—I had to master military Hebrew too. Anyone who has served in the IDF will tell you that the military has its own unique vocabulary, used only within the base's walls and in military life. Outside those fences, it just sounds like nonsense.

Shigi-digi is a light-hearted, playful way to retrain our minds for civilian speech. Instead of saying *"shekem,"* we learn to say *"makolet"* (convenience store). Instead of *"madas,"* we say *"bigdei sport"* (exercise clothes). Essentially, after years of living with the mindset and language of the IDF, before we reenter civilian life, we need to adjust so we don't look like fools wandering the streets of Tel Aviv, using vocabulary reserved only for those in olive green uniforms.

The transition from military to civilian life can be just as difficult—if not more so—than the transition from civilian to military life. Because of this, there are many programs, organizations, and government support designed to assist recently released soldiers. One day, a soldier might be in uniform in Gaza, following orders under the strict structure of the IDF, and the next suddenly free in the wide world without the same direction, routine, or structure. These programs help newly discharged soldiers find work, pursue education, and provide benefits like free public transportation for a year and assistance finding housing. There's an understanding that if the state borrows eighteen-year-olds for nearly three years to serve it, then the state has a responsibility to help these twenty-one-year-olds succeed once they cut their military ID card.

I completed my mandatory service on January 3, 2024, but for the next two and a half months, I remained with my team in Gaza as a reserve soldier. By mid-March, the time was right to return my gun, stand before my team, and cut my *choger*. While my combat role in the war was behind me, the challenges ahead were just beginning.

Suddenly, literally overnight, I went from being a soldier inside Gaza, carrying a machine gun and facing the threat of terrorists, to a civilian in the open world—with no structure, routine, or clear path. The challenges were only just beginning. My plan was eventually to move back to the United States, where my family lived and where I grew up. But I didn't want to leave Israel so quickly. After nearly half a year of war, during which I hadn't seen many friends or relatives, I wanted to properly close this chapter by spending a few months reconnecting before rushing back to New York.

Just days after my release, I was offered an opportunity to fly home to New York on a highly subsidized ticket. Understanding the opportunity's value, I decided to fly back at the end of March, see my family for a bit, and then return to Israel in early summer to spend more time with friends and relatives, just as I had planned.

But before flying home, I had one important stop to make: a visit to Be'eri. My host father from Erez knew someone from Be'eri and arranged the visit. For me, this was a chance to piece together everything that had happened on that chaotic day—and the days after. There had been many moments when I was running from place to place, but now, returning, I was finally able to understand where I had been and connect the dots in my and my unit's story.

Walking through Be'eri was shocking and surreal. In nearly half a year, barely any progress had been made toward reconstruction. The community was in a state of waiting—waiting for the hostages to return, waiting for clarity on what would come next. Who would live here? Who would come back? Who would replace the families who were murdered? Did they even want to live here anymore? These questions hung heavy over the residents.

As I walked around the kibbutz, I pictured myself months earlier, caught in the most intense moments of my life. The man guiding us was a Be'eri resident who asked me what unit I served in. I told him I was in the 890th Battalion of the Paratrooper Brigade. With a small smile, he said it was soldiers from my unit who rescued him and his family that dark Saturday. Whether it was my team or another, knowing this filled me with pride—for at least that moment. I could see the impact of our work firsthand and understand that this man might not have survived without the efforts of my battalion. That knowledge, no doubt, gave him even more reason to accompany me on the walk and revisit this difficult place together.

After this meaningful visit, I spent another week in Israel before flying home. Returning to New York was exciting, though honestly, I wasn't sure what to expect. From the moment I landed, I got a glimpse of what my welcome home would look like. At the airport, I saw my family holding a sign and smiling, and next to them was a group of yeshiva students singing classic Jewish and Zionist songs, accompanied by a guy playing guitar. Apparently, this group comes to Newark Airport every time a Lone Soldier arrives, singing to welcome them back from the war. I was truly—and utterly—shocked. Right there in the middle of the airport, these students sang "Am Yisrael Chai" by Eyal Golan as I walked out of baggage claim. It was a deeply heartwarming welcome.

Feeling the embrace of family and friends was special. Though beyond excessive and frankly unnecessary, it was the kind of hero's welcome you usually only see in movies about soldiers coming home. While it was nice, I didn't feel I deserved it. There were still soldiers fighting and hostages held in Gaza. The praise felt premature until this nightmare ended. Still, I understood where everyone was coming from. For my friends, family, and community, my return was the closest point of connection to what was happening in our homeland.

Several weeks after returning home, I spoke with my local rabbi about the possibility of sharing my story at the synagogue where I grew up. Soon after, I reached out to my principal from the Schechter School of Long Island to do the same. Once dates were set for both, I put together a presentation that accurately and succinctly told my story—everything from my enlistment to October 7th, and from my time in Gaza to my friend Omer Neutra. I delivered this presentation in front of my synagogue congregation and to students at my old school.

I found great meaning in this, and as the presentation gained attention, I began connecting with other communities throughout Long Island and beyond. Before long, I was being invited to speak at synagogues, schools, youth groups, colleges, federations, and more. The opportunity to share my story and talk with Jews—and non-Jews as well—about the situation in Israel gave me immense pride and a deep sense of connection to the ongoing war, even while I was in the United States. These speaking engagements became something I continue to give even to this day.

During the two months I was home in April and May 2024, I spoke at over fifteen venues, mainly synagogues on Long Island, and a few down in Florida when I visited my Savta Syl. At the end of May, I booked my flight back to Israel for a two-month visit through the end of July—a period I saw as a time to close a chapter of my life. This trip would give me the chance to see friends and relatives I hadn't seen in a while and to reflect on a chapter that had shaped me profoundly.

Most importantly, though, this return to Israel was about reconnecting with my friends from the army. While my service had ended, many of my friends were still serving. When I returned, they had just come back from operating inside the Gaza Strip after a two-month break. So, without a doubt, the most important thing for me was to spend time with my IDF friends during their breaks from Gaza.

One weekday in mid-to-late June, when my IDF friends were given a few days' break at home, a few of us decided to meet up at a friend's house in Tekoa, watch a movie, have a barbecue, and just hang out. Tekoa is in the West Bank, south of Jerusalem, and getting there from Tel Aviv was a bit of a challenge. Luckily, my friend Yair Avitan was driving to Tekoa from Ra'anana, a city north of Tel Aviv. That morning, I took a bus to his house, and with his mother by his side, they both made me a little Israeli breakfast before we hit the road. I remember them discussing the Haredi draft law and whether Haredim should enlist—a pretty heavy topic over a light breakfast. Soon after, we were off.

Yair and I spent the entire day together. By evening, other friends from the army were meeting up in Herzliya by the marina, so we headed back west to join them. An old friend who now works for a sailing company at the marina agreed to take us out onto the Mediterranean. With a six-pack of beer and friends from the army, we spent quality time together in the middle of the water, enjoying the lit-up coastline of Israel. Later, back on shore, Yair and I went to another friend's place near Netanya, where we hung out and closed the night sitting, talking, and relaxing in civilian clothes—not IDF uniforms. Way past midnight, we finally called it a night and went our separate ways.

This would be the last time I'd see my friend Yair Avitan.

A week later, my team reentered Gaza after more than a week-and-a-half break. I had just landed in Spain for a two-week vacation with my sister. On that Friday night, I got a call from a friend from the army. I was a bit shocked—he keeps Shabbat, and calling on Friday night wasn't usual. Picking up the phone in the middle of a main street in Barcelona, excited to hear from him, I told him to switch to FaceTime so I could show him where I was. In a serious tone, he declined and stayed on the line. Then he told me something I wasn't prepared for: as my team reentered Shejaiya in northern Gaza that day, Yair had been shot and killed on the spot. Yair Avitan took his last breath on June 28, 2024.

I was in shock. I told my sister we had to get back to the hotel, and after that, I had little energy for anything. Avitan—we called him by his last name—was the smile and joy of our team. He began his military service in Egoz, an elite commando unit, but after not making the cut, he joined us in the paratroopers toward the end of training. From the moment he joined, I knew he was special—not the biggest, tallest, or strongest guy, but with one of the biggest hearts. In contrast to many of the tough Israelis on our team, Avitan's warm and welcoming energy stood out, and he became one of my closest friends. He was one of the few army friends I hung out with outside of base, including that week before he fell in battle.

One of my greatest memories of Avitan was back in Hebron, when we were asked one night to man an outpost alone while the rest of the team went on a mission. We took turns guarding, but he insisted I get more sleep while he stood watch—a small, unnecessary gesture, but so characteristic of him. A few weeks after that, during a break from the army, Avitan, another friend, and I took a trip up north. It was the middle of July, and we set up a tent along the Kinneret (Sea of Galilee), where we swam, cooked a barbecue, and spent the night. Eleven months later, Avitan was killed in Gaza.

After June 28, devastated beyond belief, the Avitan family found ways to share their son with the world. Through events, runs, and stickers placed all over Israel and beyond, Yair Avitan's memory lives on. His mother, Einat, started an initiative to prepare food and barbecues for my company whenever we were on break from combat. As she says, "I have lost my son, but I have gained a whole company of sons." After I returned from Spain a few weeks later, and with my team leaving Gaza, Einat helped organize a big celebration to honor them before they returned to combat.

Yair Avitan's loss became a turning point for my friends and me. Up until then, we considered ourselves lucky. Hundreds of soldiers had been killed in combat since the October 7th attack, and several units had teams half wiped out in single incidents. We, however, had been spared—until Avitan. Since his death, no other soldier in my battalion has been killed. Several were injured, some severely, but no others lost. Avitan, who always had a smile on his face, certainly has a smile now as he looks down on us from above.

Leaving Israel a few weeks later, the loss of my friend was still raw. As I headed back to the United States, I already understood that I would soon feel a sense of disconnection growing stronger than before. Returning home brought its own challenges. The biggest question on my mind was simple yet overwhelming: *What do I do now?*

When I had come home a few months earlier, I knew my time was temporary—I would be heading back to Israel soon. Visiting Israel felt like a vacation, a chapter closing, a time to relax, hang out with friends, and enjoy life. But returning to New York, the stakes felt different. Now, it was time to focus.

On top of the mental stress from my military service, my body was also suffering. Carrying over one hundred pounds of gear for months in Gaza had taken a serious toll on me—long before the war, even training and exercises had worn me down. After finishing my service, I started having persistent back problems that put me into the biggest slump of my life. As someone who's always been active and passionate about sports, suddenly being restricted physically was devastating. For months, I went to physical therapy, saw a chiropractor, consulted an orthopedic surgeon, and even received multiple injections in my back. Running, lifting weights, playing sports—all were off-limits.

This physical limitation brought a level of stress I hadn't anticipated. I simply wasn't myself anymore. I went about six months without lifting weights and nearly nine months without running. When I finally started to get back into it, the pain was still there, but it gradually lessened. Today, my back still aches and bothers me, but not enough to keep me from being active.

Still, my situation is far from unique. IDF combat service—especially during wartime—places enormous strain on the body. Thousands of soldiers have been officially recorded as combat-injured, but many more, like me, bear the invisible scars from the relentless physical demands of combat. These lasting effects will stay with us long after the fighting ends. While I can still exercise, I know my back issues will likely follow me for life—and my military service is a major cause.

Dealing with my back issues while adjusting to life back in the United States made figuring out my next steps a big challenge. Waiting for things to fall into place required a lot of patience. One thing I knew for sure was that I would continue my speaking engagements. Without an official job or the ability to exercise fully, these speaking opportunities gave me something meaningful to focus on and work toward. Beyond that, my main priority was finding employment.

After returning from Israel, I wanted to find work connected to what I had just experienced. Naturally, I looked toward the Jewish world. After several agonizing months of applications, interviews, and waiting, I finally landed a position with the UJA Federation of New York as a development assistant on their Wall Street and Financial Services team. While it might seem like a small step, for me it was a huge moment. Nearly eight months since completing my military service, living with little routine and no exercise, I desperately needed structure—and I found it at UJA.

For the first time since cutting my military ID card, I was finally working again. To me, this marked the beginning of a new chapter. Until that point, I was still living in the shadow of the previous chapter—one filled with war, hardship, and hostages still held in Gaza. Now, I could finally focus on an exciting next step.

A few months after starting at UJA in Manhattan, I moved into the Upper West Side—a beautiful neighborhood in New York City with a large Jewish community. Despite all the challenges and hardships of life after IDF service, things were finally starting to come together. Best of all, I was able to exercise again and slowly regain my physical strength.

While I continue to move further away from my IDF service, I know there is still a long road ahead. My service, especially the war, will remain etched in my mind forever. The moments of October 7th, when I saw my life flash before my eyes, are memories ingrained deep within me. How could I ever forget?

I'm often reminded by family and friends that the effects of trauma, characterized as posttraumatic stress disorder—or PTSD—sometimes don't show up until long after an event. Since the war, I haven't experienced PTSD, but I also know I shouldn't dismiss the possibility or act like I'm somehow above it. I started seeing a therapist while I was home, and many of my friends from the service have done the same. Thankfully, the stigma around mental health is slowly fading in the United States, and the importance of taking care of yourself—even if you don't think you need it—is now better understood. That stigma remains stronger in Israel, but if there's one silver lining from this war, it's that mental health awareness has grown considerably there. The nation sees itself as a country in trauma, and everyone—from released hostages, soldiers, and evacuated residents of the Gaza Envelope to ordinary civilians—has sought mental health support. Many soldiers in my company have also started therapy because, even if they don't feel they need it right now, they understand it's the right and responsible step.

Together with my IDF friends, we continue to focus on taking care of ourselves—both physically and mentally—as we move forward from military life into civilian life.

Life after the war has been unique, full of ups and downs, challenges and triumphs. What might seem ironic to many of you reading this, life after the war has felt harder than the war itself. During the war, the structure, routine, and deep sense of purpose gave my life a meaning I had never experienced before. After cutting my card, I lost that structure and had to find a new purpose. My speaking engagements and writing this book have helped fill that void, but it's still a work in progress. As

I continue my journey, the memories from my service will always be a part of me. The challenges of life after service will remain too, and I will keep learning, growing, and moving forward with them.

EPILOGUE

Kiryat Shaul Cemetery, Tel Aviv, November 7, 2025

I boarded the plane at Newark International Airport and began the most spontaneous journey of my life. While an American enlisting in the IDF is quite crazy, there was nothing spontaneous about that decision or journey. This, however, was.

My friend Omer finally came home. After 758 days, Omer came home. He didn't come home as we wanted, but we were 99.9 percent sure he wouldn't. Eleven months earlier the IDF confirmed Omer was killed on October 7, 2023, and since then, his body had been held as a bargaining chip by Hamas. We didn't want to believe the news that he was dead and a sliver of our hearts still believed he would come back alive. Deep down, though, we knew this wouldn't happen, but we kept hoping anyway.

Omer's body was returned to Israel on Sunday, November 2, 2025. The funeral was scheduled for that Friday, November 7, in Israel, at the Kiryat Shaul military cemetery outside Tel Aviv.

I spent that Monday processing the news. That evening, I was asked to speak at a gathering at Columbus Circle in New York City, honoring the hero who just returned home. I shared about my friend Omer and spoke of how he continues to inspire Jews throughout the world every day. At Columbus Circle, friends of Omer discussed trying to get to Israel in any way they could for the funeral. I knew I had to as well.

The next morning, I picked up my phone. I started calling, texting, and reaching out to anyone and everyone who could help. I got a call back, "I think I have a ticket for you."

I was connected to someone else, who connected me to a generous donor, an amazing person who wanted to sponsor a ticket for a friend of Omer to attend his funeral. I couldn't believe it.

The next day I boarded a plane and flew halfway around the world.

There was no expectation for me to attend the funeral, and no reason I had to. The reason was for me. I wanted to be there. I also knew that the Neutras, seeing how many friends flew across the world for his funeral, would feel the love they so deserved.

So, I landed in Israel, and three days later I was already flying home. A quick visit, but a visit with a purpose.

Friday morning, November 7, I woke up and joined the Neutras with family and friends in Ra'anana where the casket resided, and where the procession to the funeral would begin. Boarding buses, we slowly drove down the main street in Ra'anana, as the sidewalks on both sides were filled with thousands of Israelis holding Israeli flags and signs honoring Omer. The procession lasted just over twenty minutes, and my sight was fixated on the scenes outside. The respect and honor felt was something I can't express. In no other country do I think this would happen. In no other military would this happen. Omer received a hero's procession.

Arriving at the cemetery, Omer's casket was removed and carried to his final resting place. We all walked behind him. After he was placed in the ground, we poured sacks of dirt over him. Burying him in the earth he came from, in the land he gave his life to protect.

The cemetery was packed, filled in all directions. In attendance were major Israeli generals, former politicians, famous Israeli singers such as Ishay Ribo, Israel's President Isaac Herzog, the head of the US Central Command Admiral Brad Cooper, friends from Israel and the United States, and his loving family. Many spoke, and everyone cried. Wreaths were placed on Omer's grave. Respect was given to him. Honor given to a hero.

Less than two days later, I boarded a plane at Ben Gurion International Airport, returned to New York, took a NJ Transit train back to Manhattan, and went to work the next day. As if none of it happened. As if I just dreamed it. Less than three days in Israel, attending my friend's funeral, and now just like several days prior, back to the routine of life.

I felt incredibly fortunate. I was lucky. The funeral was sad, this was all sad, burying a friend, a twenty-one-year-old, is sad. This is also what we wanted, what we were fighting for. With almost complete certainty we knew Omer was no longer alive, and we had eleven months to process it. We fought for the return not of Omer, but of his body, and thankfully, that day came, and the funeral we all prayed for happened. To pray that a funeral happens is a messed-up reality, but it's a reality we have become accustomed to since October 7th.

As I neared the completion of this book, I wondered, *Will Omer's body be returned by the time it is ready to be published?* How could I finish a book about this chapter of my life without knowing if or when Omer was returned to Israel? Thankfully, those questions have been answered. My spontaneous three-day trip to Israel, and Omer's funeral, brought a degree of closure to his family and friends but importantly for me as well, and seems a fitting way to end this book.

MAPS

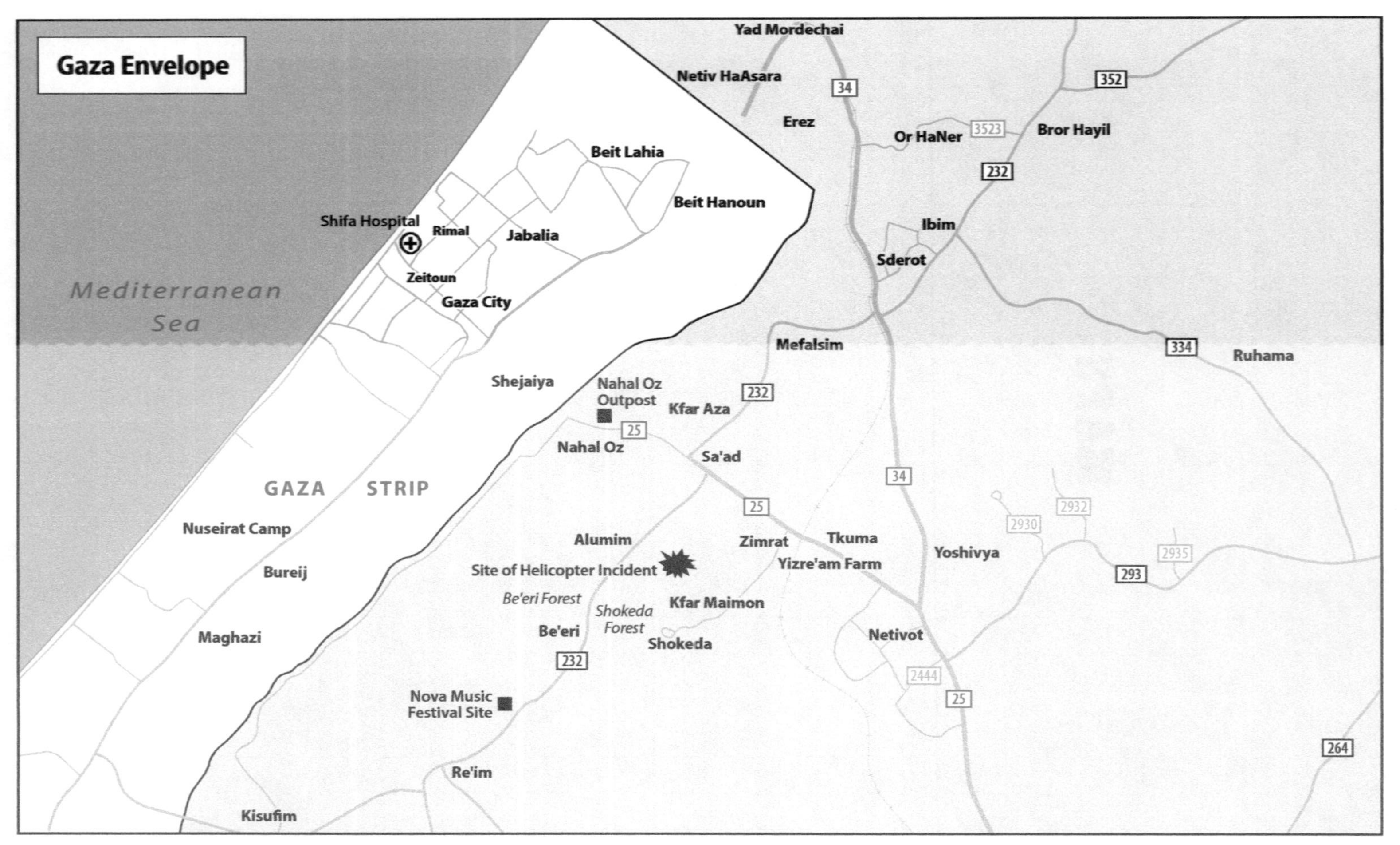
Gaza Envelope
Mediterranean Sea
Yad Mordechai
Netiv HaAsara
Erez
Beit Lahia
Beit Hanoun
Shifa Hospital
Rimal
Zeitoun
Jabalia
Gaza City
Or HaNer
Bror Hayil
Ibim
Sderot
Shejaiya
Nahal Oz Outpost
Kfar Aza
Nahal Oz
Sa'ad
Mefalsim
GAZA STRIP
Nuseirat Camp
Bureij
Maghazi
Alumim
Site of Helicopter Incident
Be'eri Forest
Be'eri
Shokeda Forest
Kfar Maimon
Shokeda
Zimrat
Tkuma
Yizre'am Farm
Yoshivya
Netivot
Nova Music Festival Site
Re'im
Kisufim
Ruhama
352
34
232
334
293
25
264
232
232
3523
2935
2932
2930
2444

The Focal Points of Battles and Events in Kibbutz Be'eri

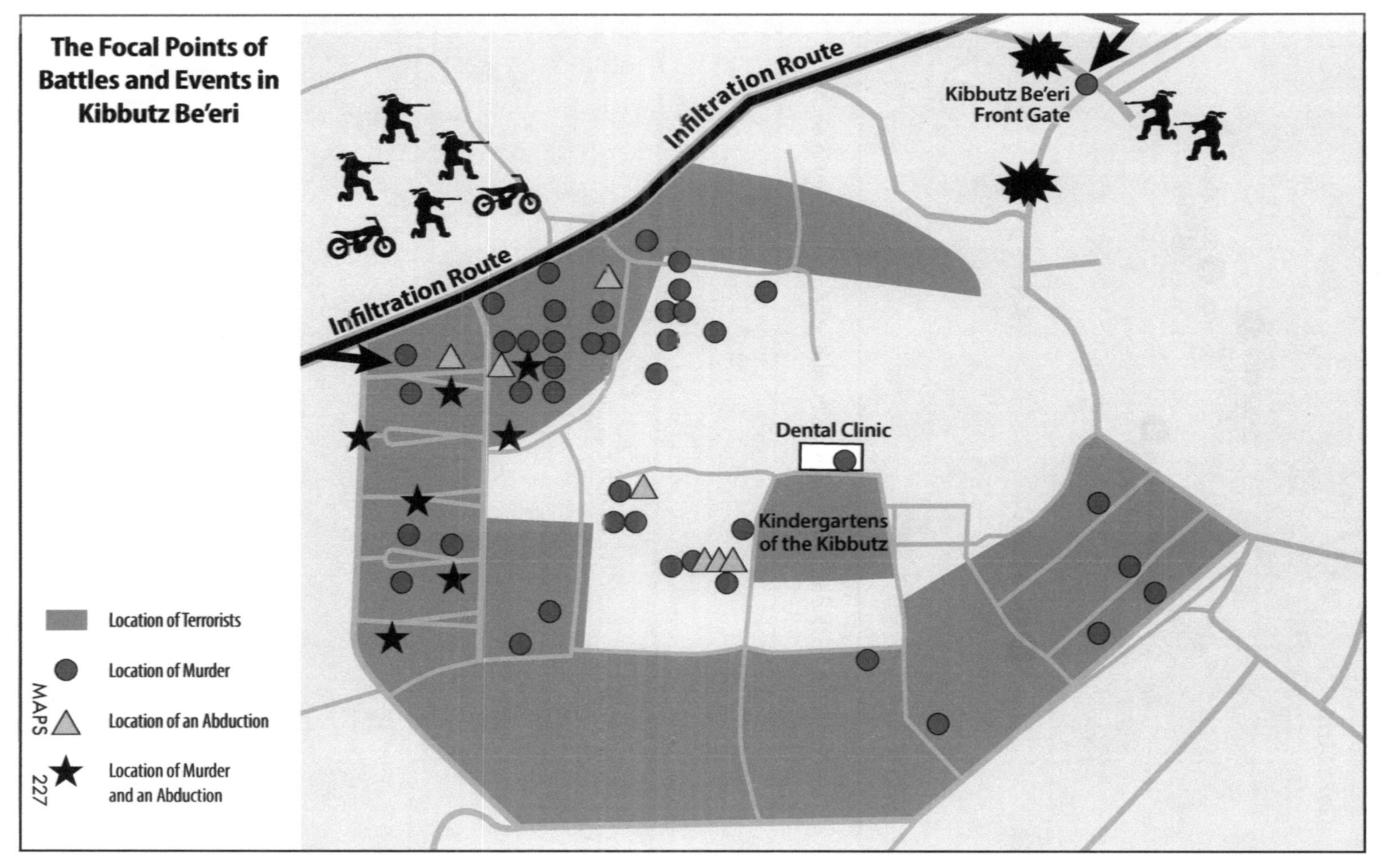

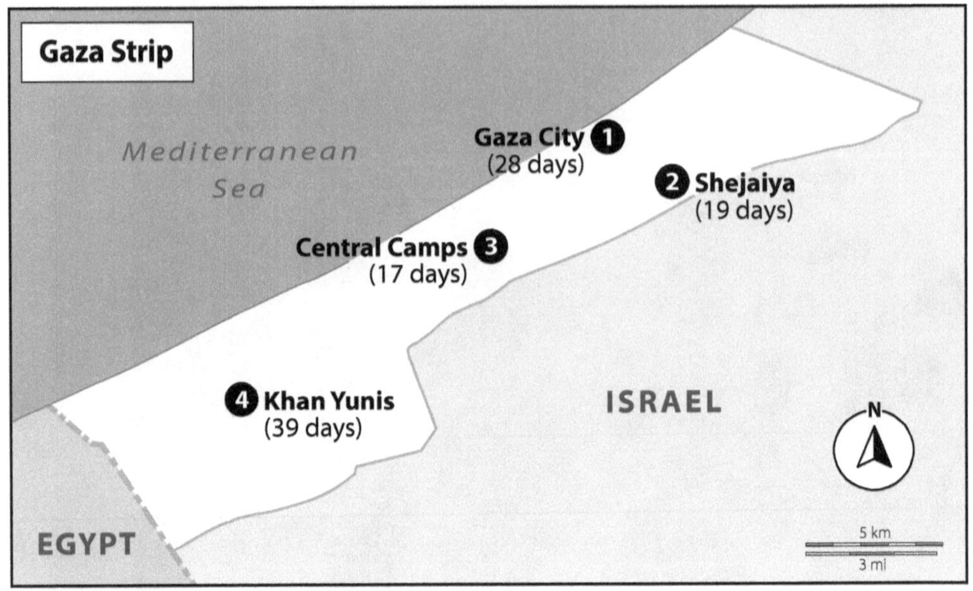

Days depicted on this map represent the number of days Ira spent in each part of Gaza.

PHOTOGRAPHS

In helicopter en route to Gaza Envelope on October 7th
Courtesy Ira Kohler

Aliya flight [From left to right: Beth (mother), Jeremy (brother), Ira, Shira (sister), Michael (father)]

Courtesy Ira Kohler

My host family attending my Beret Ceremony

Courtesy Beret Ceremony Official Photographer

Receiving the Paratrooper Red Beret
Beret Ceremony Official Photographer

Training with Negev
Courtesy Ira Kohler

Nebi Musa Training Base, days before October 7th attack
Courtesy Ira Kohler

Preparing equipment for War Week (Targad)

Courtesy Ira Kohler

Helicopter hit by rocket
and on fire
Courtesy Ira Kohler

Helicopter destroyed
Courtesy ynet

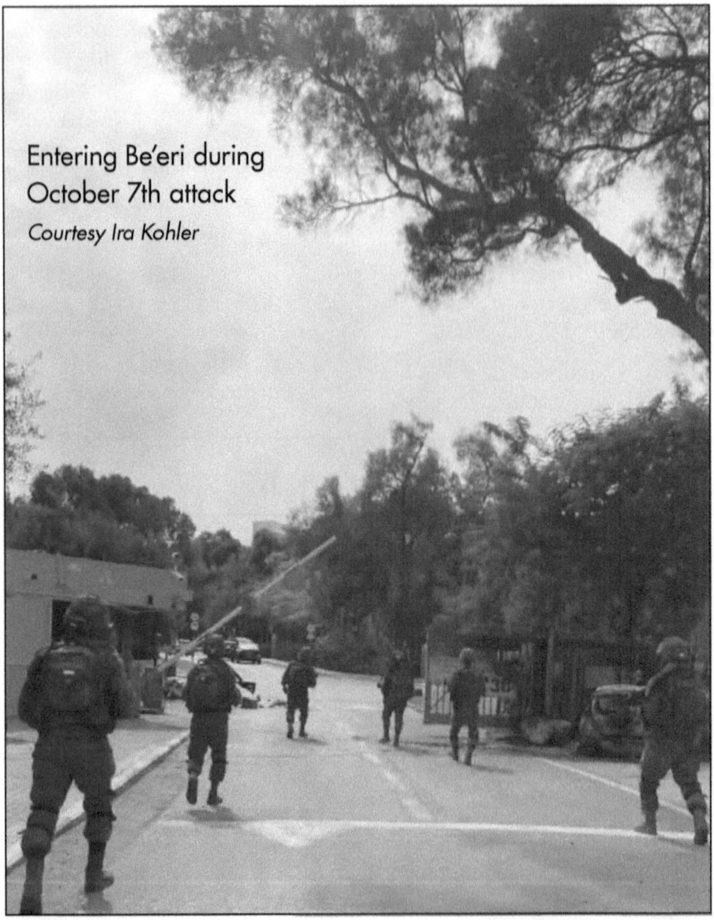

Entering Be'eri during October 7th attack

Courtesy Ira Kohler

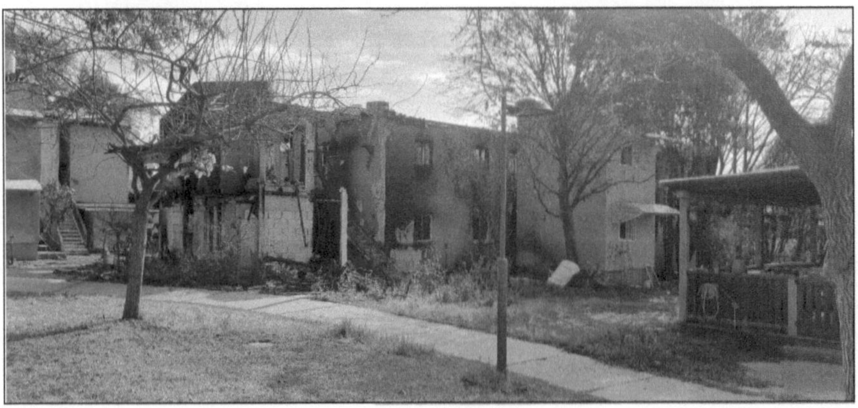

Burnt house in Be'eri where we rescued a family

Courtesy Eli B.

Walking on Gaza beach
Courtesy Ira Kohler

Team after leaving Shejaiya
Courtesy Ira Kohler

Receiving my birthday cake in Gaza
Courtesy Or H.

Meeting Israeli singer Idan Amedi
Courtesy Beth W.

Playing cards in Gaza
Courtesy Or H.

Omer and me as children
Courtesy Orna N.

Attending Omer's Commander ceremony with my parents
Courtesy Ira Kohler

The last time I saw Omer
Courtesy Orna N.

Cutting my *choger*
Courtesy Ira Kohler

Speaking on Long Island at a rally marking the six-month anniversary of the October 7th attack

Courtesy Ira Kohler

With my friend Yair Avitan (on the right)

Courtesy Ira Kohler

ACKNOWLEDGMENTS

Once a Paratrooper is my memoir—an American Jew who grew up in the suburbs of New York City and, fueled by a love of Israel, decided to enlist in the IDF and protect his country. However, this story is more than just about me; this story represents an entire people: a people fighting for two thousand years to come home, and a people continually fighting to keep that home alive.

The title *Once a Paratrooper* is inspired by the IDF Paratrooper slogan "Once a paratrooper, always a paratrooper." Anyone who has ever served as a paratrooper in the IDF remains one long after they finish their service. This title also indicates that my memoir is reflective, as I tell my story after it happened, while acknowledging that I am continually shaped by the moments and lessons of my service.

The cover photo also has great meaning to me. Taken on October 7th, it captures my unit walking into Kibbutz Be'eri. A commander on our team snapped that photo moments before we crossed the kibbutz gate and entered into a place that would change our lives forever.

I'd first like to thank the brave men and women of the IDF who right now are standing on our borders protecting Israel. Every time I entered Gaza, I'd hear one phrase repeatedly: *Tachzeru B'Shalom*; "May you come home in peace." May every soldier currently serving, both in their active and reserve service, return in peace to their loved ones.

Throughout the writing and production of this book, there are a tremendous number of individuals to thank, and the most important are my friends in the IDF. These friends understand me in ways that nobody else ever can. They fought alongside me on October 7th, for over 100 days in Gaza, and many are continuing reserve duty to this day. Furthermore, in the production of this book, many of my friends served as companions to talk my work through, recount stories together, and help sharpen my memories of what we witnessed together during the crazy events of October 7th. I thank them all for their service, their continued service, and their partnership in this project.

This book could not have been completed without the professional expertise of GMK Writing and Editing, Inc. I'd like to thank Randy Landenheim-Gil for serving as my development editor, Kelly Clody as my copy editor, Katie Benoit as manager of this project, Vicky Shea for designing the cover and interior of the book, Elizabeth Crooks for proofreading, Libby Kingsbury for laying out the book, and, most importantly, Gary Krebs for leading the way and providing a tremendous amount of guidance and support throughout this process. Everything from the editing, design, and production was made possible by GMK Writing and Editing, Inc., and this book could not have been completed without all their support.

In writing my book, I was looking for a partner to sponsor my work, and I am fortunate to have found this in the Bring Omer Home, Inc. organization. Initially, Bring Omer Home, Inc. raised funds to fight for Omer's release, and after his body was returned to Israel on November 2nd, 2025, the organization shifted its focus to preserving Omer's legacy. *Once a Paratrooper* tells the story of both Omer and me, our love of Israel, and why we both decided to enlist in the IDF, as well as powerfully preserves Omer's legacy, which is now the goal of the organization.

I'd also like to thank Orna and Ronen Neutra for their partnership throughout this process. I appreciate their guidance as I wrote about Omer and his story, and I'd like to thank them for writing the foreword to my book. Their support proved invaluable as I neared the completion of this project.

To support my book, I am grateful to all the incredible individuals who took the time to read my memoir and write a meaningful endorsement. A special thanks to Major General (Res.) Doron Almog, Chairman of the Executive of The Jewish Agency for Israel and Chairman of ADI Negev-Nahalat Eran, for writing the Opening Remarks to my book.

While fighting in the war, my community of friends and family throughout the world gave me motivation to push forward. My parents created a WhatsApp group called "Friends of Ira" to share updates about me, and at its peak this group reached over 600 people. I am incredibly grateful for this community, and I thank them for their support while I was in Gaza, as well as their support now as I share my book with the world.

Lastly, I'd like to thank my loving family. My father, Michael, helped serve as a springboard for ideas and helped edit the book countless times. Thank you for your support throughout this entire process. My mother, Beth, sparked creativity in the book and in its publicity. She always thought outside the box, helping spawn ideas to create an even better finished product. To my brother Jeremy, sister Shira, and my entire extended family, thank you for all your love and support throughout this entire process. You are all the backbone of this incredible work.

I am incredibly grateful for amazing family, friends, and professionals who helped turn this idea into a finished book, and I am hoping this story helps share the love of Israel and of the Jewish people that I hold so close to my heart.

ABOUT THE AUTHOR

Courtesy Moyses M.

Ira Kohler served in the IDF's 890th Battalion of the Paratrooper Brigade. Originally from Plainview, Long Island, he attended the University of Delaware, graduating with a BA in economics. Several months later, he moved to Israel. Serving as a Lone Soldier, Ira enlisted in January 2022. On October 7, 2023, he found himself in the heart of Israel's hardest battles as he fought in Kibbutz Be'eri. From there, Ira went on to serve over one hundred days inside the Gaza Strip. Upon completing his service, Ira moved back to the United States and became a noted public speaker.

Courtesy Bring Omer Home, Inc.

Bring Omer Home, Inc.

ABOUT THE CHARITY

Captain Omer Maxim Neutra *Z"L*, was kidnapped and taken hostage by Hamas terrorists on October 7, 2023, along with more than 250 others. After 758 long days, Omer was returned home to Israel and laid to rest in the land he loved and defended. While the mission to bring Omer home has ended, the responsibility that grew around his name has not.

Bring Omer Home is focused on preserving Omer's legacy—the way he lived and the values he embodied. The organization supports educational, leadership, and values-based initiatives inspired by Omer's life and works to ensure that the stories of the hostages and their families are never forgotten.

We invite you to support this effort and help ensure that Omer is remembered for how he lived—with responsibility, leadership, and care for the people around him—and that those values continue to matter.

Visit: https://www.gofundme.com/f/join-the-fight-to-free-omer-neutra